NECESSARY
SKILLS
AND THEN SOME...

DK

LONDON, NEW YORK, MELBOURNE, MUNICH, AND DELHI

Senior editors Francesca Baines, Carron Brown, Jenny Finch
Senior designers Sheila Collins, Stefan Podhorodecki
Editors Steven Carton, Clare Hibbert, James Mitchem
Art editors Angela Ball, David Ball, Mik Gates, Ralph Pitchford
Designers Katie Knutton, Hoa Luc

Managing editor Linda Esposito
Managing art editor Jim Green
Category publisher Laura Buller

Commissioned illustrations Acute, Jelly, Maltings Partnership
Picture research Rob Nunn
Production editor Marc Staples
Senior production controller Angela Graef
Jacket designer Yumiko Tahata
Jacket editor Matilda Gollon
Development team Hazel Martin, Joanna Pocock
Design development manager Sophia M. Tampakopoulos Turner

This edition published in 2014
First published in the United States in 2010 by
DK Publishing, 345 Hudson Street,
New York, New York 10014

Copyright © 2010, 2014 Dorling Kindersley Limited

Previously published as *This Book Made Me Do It* (2010)

001–257311–Sep/14

DK books are available at special discounts when purchased in bulk for
sales promotions, premiums, fund-raising, or educational use. For details, contact:
DK Publishing Special Markets, 345 Hudson Street, New York, New York 10014
or SpecialSales@dk.com

A catalog record for this book is available from the Library of Congress.

ISBN: 978-1-4654-2763-2

High-res workflow proofed by MDP, UK
Printed and bound in China by Hung Hing

Discover more at www.dk.com

NECESSARY SKILLS AND THEN SOME...

Written by John Woodward

Contributors: Francesca Baines,
Carron Brown, Steven Carton,
Jenny Finch, Joe Fullman,
Clare Hibbert, and James Mitchem

Illustrated by Tobatron

CONTENTS

How to use this book safely—an important note for children and adults

This book is packed with things to do—some are very simple, while others are more tricky. There are some things we hope you never have to do. With luck you'll never find yourself face-to-face with a bear, but we give you advice to reduce the odds. We've also told you what to do in a worst-case scenario. But you should never seek out a bear to check that we're right.

We've also told you how to do some extraordinary things that you've probably only dreamed about. But if we say you shouldn't try something yourself, we mean it. Don't take off in an armchair balloon, for example, as you could get arrested for entering foreign airspace.

Just use your common sense. We'd never recommend for you stroll up to the cockpit and suggest to the pilot to bring the plane into Chicago O'Hare Airport—one of us might be onboard. And it's obvious you shouldn't try your first ski jump with only this book in your hand for guidance as you stand at the top of the ramp. We hope this book will inspire you to take up a new sport or activity, but if it's in any way dangerous, you'll need to properly research it and get professional advice before you start.

Have fun reading this book and trying things for yourself sensibly and safely. We've marked with symbols where you need to take extra care and where you must have an adult to help or supervise you—see below. In most cases, it's obvious why you have to be careful, but if there's specific safety advice you need to know, we'll tell you.

The authors and publisher cannot take responsibility for the outcome, injury, loss, damage, or mess that occurs as a result of you attempting the activities in this book. Tell an adult before you do any of them, carefully follow the instructions, and look out for and pay attention to the following symbols:

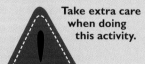 Take extra care when doing this activity.

 You should do this activity only with an adult.

 Read this information for guidance on specific safety advice.

AMAZE YOUR FRIENDS

Everyone should have a few tricks up their sleeve to surprise or entertain people when they least expect it, and it's time to learn something new! You could learn how to read a friend's palm, perform a mystifying magic trick, perfect some cool dance moves, or perhaps consider something more spectacular, like walking a tightrope. Go on—amaze yourself!

Pull a tablecloth

This classic trick never fails to amaze. Clear the dinner table in reverse by pulling the tablecloth out from underneath the items on its surface. The goal is to smoothly complete the move while the objects remain in place on the table.

TOP TIP
You can also try this trick using a stack of coins and a sheet of paper. It's not as dramatic but gives the same effect.

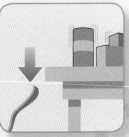

1 Place the tablecloth on a tabletop, smooth out any wrinkles, and stack your objects on top, close to the table's edge. Make sure the items aren't breakable.

2 Prepare to pull the tablecloth by firmly holding one end of it. Place one hand on each side of the overhanging cloth, parallel to the tabletop.

3 Quickly pull the tablecloth straight down from the tabletop. The faster and smoother the pull, the higher the chance of success.

For a more traditional dining-related activity,
go to pages 58–59 to learn
how to fold a napkin

HOW THIS WORKS

According to Isaac Newton's first law of motion, an object at rest will remain at rest unless acted on by an outside force. If the surface of the table is smooth and you pull hard enough on the cloth so that it moves quickly, the friction created is not a strong enough force to move the objects. This is also why the trick works better with heavier objects.

Juggle two balls . . .

Juggling is a great party trick that, when perfected, will mesmerize anyone who watches.

TOP TIP
Tired of picking up balls from the floor? Try tossing beanbags— it won't stop you from dropping them, but they won't roll away.

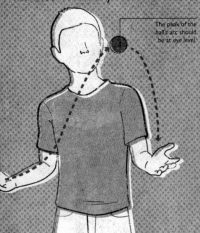

The peak of the ball's arc should be at eye level.

The ball should fall naturally into your hand.

1 Toss one ball in an arcing motion from one hand to another. Aim for the ball to peak at the same height each time you toss it.

2 Don't reach to catch the ball; let it land in your hand. Repeat this process until you can maintain a solid rhythm.

3 When the first ball is at the highest point of its arc, throw another ball from your other hand just below the arc of the first ball.

Escape from handcuffs

Become a regular Houdini and escape from imprisonment. You don't want to be tied down, so follow these steps and make a great escape.

1 Tie a loop of string around each of your friend's wrists. Then ask your friend to do the same to you, first crossing your string over theirs.

2 Pull your friend's length of string toward you and push it through the loop tied to your left wrist from back to front.

3 Bend your left hand down and push it through the loop. Then straighten out your hand, making the loop of string move to the back.

4 Pull your hands back and you will be free. Try challenging two other friends—see how long they take to figure it out!

Twirl a pencil

Astound your classmates by skillfully twirling a pencil around your thumb while deep in thought.

1 Hold a pencil between your thumb, index, and middle fingers. Your middle finger should be just below halfway up the pencil.

2 Pull your middle finger toward you and extend your index finger. Your middle finger should end up resting on your thumb.

3 The pencil will move around your thumb. When it hits your middle finger, move your index finger back to catch it.

. . . or three balls

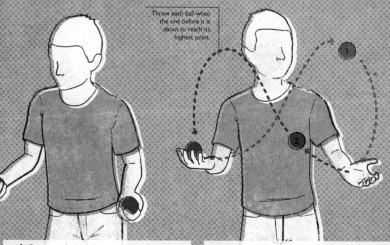

Throw each ball when the one before it is about to reach its highest point.

Once in a rhythm, you will be juggling with three balls in no time at all!

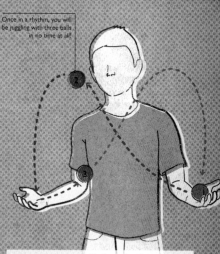

4 Once you feel ready to move on to juggling three balls, take hold of two balls in one hand and one ball in the other.

5 Start with the hand holding two balls. Throw one ball and then throw the ball in your other hand just before the first reaches its highest arc.

6 When the second ball reaches the peak of its arc, throw the third and repeat that pattern using the rhythm of two-ball juggling.

Change a card by magic

If you want to show off in front of you friends, why not impress them with a magic trick? Tell them that you can change a card just by touching it. You'll need lots of practice to make your performance perfect, but stick with it.

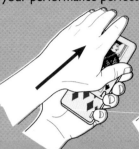

1 Place a deck of cards face up in one of your hands. Show the audience that your other hand is empty.

2 Push your palm over the deck of cards, using the top of your palm to move the top card slightly forward.

3 Keeping the cards covered, pull your palm back, bringing the second card from the top with you.

4 Slide your palm forward again, pushing the second card back to the top of the deck. Reveal the magic!

Multiply your money

Sadly, it isn't possible to double your money with magic, despite the fact that this trick will convince your friends that you can turn one small coin into two larger ones.

TOP TIP
You need to perform this trick very quickly so that your audience never sees the hidden coins.

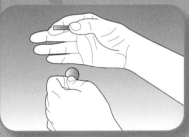

1 To prepare, place two large identical coins horizontally between the thumb and index finger of your right hand, and hold a smaller coin in your other hand.

2 Place the smaller coin vertically between your thumb and index finger, so that it obscures both of the large coins from the audience's view. This is your starting point.

3 As you bring your hands together, use your left thumb to slide the smaller coin over the others so that they are stacked with the smallest coin on top.

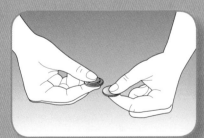
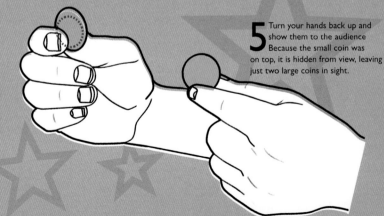

4 Quickly move the coins between your hands so that in one hand you have a large coin and in the other a large coin with the small coin hidden behind it.

5 Turn your hands back up and show them to the audience Because the small coin was on top, it is hidden from view, leaving just two large coins in sight.

Guess a friend's card

By combining some smooth hand moves with a bit of showmanship, you can misdirect an audience so that they believe you are doing one thing while you're actually doing something else.

1 This trick requires a little preparation. Pick a card, say the ace of hearts, and place it at the top of the deck. Write the name of the card on a piece of paper, fold the paper, and put in your pocket.

2 Take the deck and push the four top cards into your palm with your thumb—the ace of hearts will be at the bottom. Hold these cards slightly apart with a finger. Casually spread the other cards over the top.

3 Ask a volunteer to point to a card. Split the deck at this card, placing the top half at the bottom, but slide the four cards you are holding separately underneath.

4 Put the deck back together and reveal the bottom card to your audience—the ace of hearts! It is the card you wrote down on the piece of paper and put in your pocket, not the one your volunteer picked.

5 Reveal to your audience that you have psychic powers. Put the deck to one side, reach into your pocket and show the audience the paper with your prediction on it.

Ace of hearts

Palm a coin

Palming is a technique for concealing an object in the palm of your hand to make it look as if it has disappeared. It takes a lot of practice to master, but it's an important technique that every budding magician should learn.

The coin has been slipped into your right hand.

1 Face your audience and extend your left hand out to the side with your palm open.

2 Pinch a coin between the thumb and middle finger of your right hand and hold it up.

3 Place the coin flat in the center of the palm of your left hand, but don't let go of it.

4 Loosely close your fingers down over the coin, but pretend to hold it tightly.

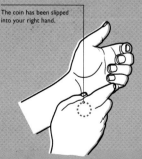

5 Pull your hand away and slip the coin into your palm so it seems to have vanished.

Saw someone in half

Despite being perhaps the most famous magic trick of all, sawing someone in half is by no means the hardest. However, it does require specialized equipment and two assistants, so you should not try this at home. But if you have ever been curious as to how it's pulled off, now you'll know!

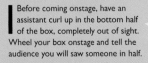

1 Before coming onstage, have an assistant curl up in the bottom half of the box, completely out of sight. Wheel your box onstage and tell the audience you will saw someone in half.

2 Ask a second assistant to get inside the box. They should curl their body so that they remain in only the top half of the box. Never let the audience see inside, though.

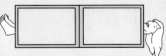

3 At exactly the same time, the hidden assistant should put their legs through the hole in the bottom so that it looks like only one person is lying down in the box.

4 Saw through the box and pull the two sections apart. After your audience gasps, bring the halves back together. The hidden assistant should pull their legs in just as you help the other assistant out of the box.

Repair a string with magic

Like many magic tricks, this one requires preparation. The key is never revealing that there is more than one piece of string. To distract your audience from exactly what is going on, make sure your performance is a showstopper with grand gestures and captivating commentary.

1 Before you begin, take a short length of string and make it into a loop. Tape the ends together. Keep this string concealed in your hand, held as shown above.

2 Hold a length of string up to the audience in your other hand, showing it is a single piece. Taking it in the middle, place it into your first hand, with the loop at the top.

3 Push the string about halfway into your palm so that the strands hang out of the bottom. Then pull the top of your hidden loop out of the top of your hand.

4 Ask a volunteer to assist you by cutting the loop sticking out of your hand. Tell your audience that you will be able to repair the string with magic.

5 Wave your hand over the rope, obscuring your audience's view, and tuck the broken loop out of sight into your palm. Then pull the "repaired" string out of the bottom of your palm.

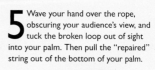

Learn to tie more effective knots on pages 148–149

TOP TIP
Say some magic words to divert your audience's attention to somewhere other than the hand hiding the string.

15

Twist some fun balloon shapes

Balloon modeling is a fun party trick, and there are lots of different shapes to make. Here are three of the most popular. The only things you'll need are balloons and a lot of puffs—or a small pump!

Types of balloons

Modeling balloons come in several sizes. The most common, and the size needed to make these models, is called 260. Find them in party stores or on the Internet.

Sword

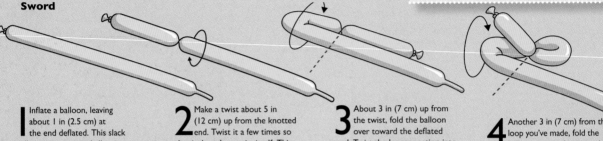

1 Inflate a balloon, leaving about 1 in (2.5 cm) at the end deflated. This slack allows you to twist balloons without bursting them.

2 Make a twist about 5 in (12 cm) up from the knotted end. Twist it a few times so that it doesn't untwist itself. This will be the sword's handle.

3 About 3 in (7 cm) up from the twist, fold the balloon over toward the deflated end. Twist the longer section into the first twist to make a loop.

4 Another 3 in (7 cm) from the loop you've made, fold the balloon over and twist in the same place for a second loop.

Kissing swans

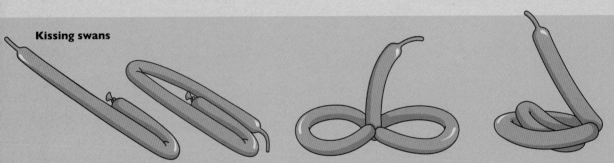

1 Inflate a balloon, leaving a 4-in (10-cm) tail. About 8 in (20 cm) up from the knotted end, make a fold.

2 Fold the tail again so that the end meets the first fold. It should look a little like a paper clip.

3 Twist all three parts together where they meet, making sure you catch the knot in the twist. You should have two loops and a long tube sticking up from the middle.

4 Now take one of the loops and tuck it into the other to make the swan's body. The upright tube will form its neck and head.

Poodle

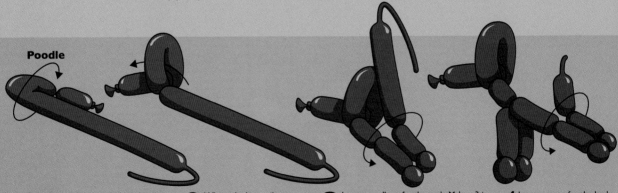

1 Blow up and tie your balloon, leaving an 7-in (18-cm) tail. Twist a 2-in (5-cm) bubble for the head and then make a fold about 2 in (5 cm) away.

2 Where the long tail meets the twist, fold together to make a loop. Push the head through this loop.

3 Leave a small gap for the neck. Make a 3-in (7-cm) bubble, then two 1-in (2.5-cm) bubbles, and another 3-in (7-cm) bubble. Twist the last twist into the first twist.

4 Leave a space for the body about 3 in (7 cm) long and then repeat step 3 to make the poodle's hind legs.

5 Straighten out the hilt and the longest section of balloon—the blade—so that they are in line with each other. En garde!

5 Fold the top of the neck down, away from the body. Hold it tightly and squeeze some of the air around the bend you've made. Repeat to give the swan a mate.

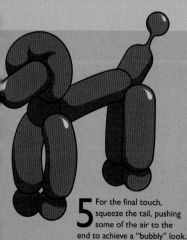

5 For the final touch, squeeze the tail, pushing some of the air to the end to achieve a "bubbly" look.

Take to the skies

Have you ever wondered if it is possible to achieve liftoff with balloons? Well, using strong weather balloons made of latex and filled with helium, it is. Tie some to a chair and you could hitch a ride.

1 Secure a lightweight chair to a launching area clear of anything overhead, using strong rope. Prepare any provisions that you'd like to take with you.

2 Attach a bunch of weather balloons to the chair and fill them with helium. Once they are inflated, get in the chair and strap yourself in.

3 Have your friends cut the ropes so that you soar into the air. Enjoy the view!

4 To come back down to earth, cut some of the balloon strings. Do this gradually so that you have a slow, controlled descent.

Safety!
While several people have completed a lawn-chair flight, do not try this at home. It is very dangerous and strictly for the professionals!

Make an invincible balloon

This simple trick will leave your audience stumped as to how you've pushed a real pin into a real balloon without making it go pop.

Go to pages 106–107 and blow some brilliant bubbles.

1 Blow up a balloon and stick two pieces of tape about 1 in (2 cm) over it in a few different places. Make sure that it sticks on completely flat to reduce visibility.

2 Holding the balloon so that it faces you, push some pins into the balloon through the pieces of tape. The tape will stop the balloon from bursting.

3 Carefully take out the pins and prove that the balloon and pins are not fake by throwing the balloon up into the air so that it lands on a pin and pops.

Find magic number 9

Before you start, bear in mind the answer is always 9, so if you do this trick in front of a group of friends, you'll be able to do it only once. And obviously don't tell your friends the name of the trick or you'll give the game away!

1 Write the number 9 on a piece of paper. Fold the piece of paper and give it to a friend, telling him not to look at it.

2 With a calculator, get your friend to do the following calculations:

- start with his age
- add the number of his house
- add the last four digits of his phone number
- add the number of pets he owns . . .
- . . . and the number of brothers and sisters he has
- then multiply the result by 18
- add the digits of the answer together. If the answer still has more than one digit, ask him to keep adding the digits together until there is only one.

3 The answer is always 9. Tell your friend to look at the piece of paper and watch his amazement!

Guess the domino

Use some nifty math to fool your friends into thinking you are psychic by guessing which domino they have in their hand. This trick is simple, but it works every time!

1 Give a set of dominoes to a friend. Ask her to choose a domino at random without letting you know which one she has picked.

2 Ask her to pick one of the numbers on the domino and then do the following calculations. She should multiply the number by 5, add 7, multiply by 2, and then add the other number on the domino.

3 Ask your friend to tell you the answer she arrived at. Subtract 14 from this and you will be left with a two-digit number, which will correspond to the two numbers on your friend's domino. Magic!

TOP TIP
It's fine for your friend to use a calculator for this trick. If they get their math wrong, the trick will fall flat!

Escape from a maze

Mazes are life-size puzzles that people seem to love getting lost in—as long as they can eventually find a way out! If you commit these tips to memory, you'll be out in no time at all.

A-MAZING
The word *labyrinth* is often used interchangably with *maze*, but they are not the same. A labyrinth has a single path leading to the center and back out again.

Stick to one side
A simply-connected maze is one where all of the walls are connected to the outer boundary. In a maze like this, keep one hand against one wall and follow the path. As long as you don't swap hands halfway, you will always end up at the exit.

Trial and error
Mazes where some of the walls aren't connected to one another are more difficult to solve. Trial and error is the only way—leave markers on the ground so that you know if you have doubled back. With this maze, the challenge is to find your way to the center and then out again.

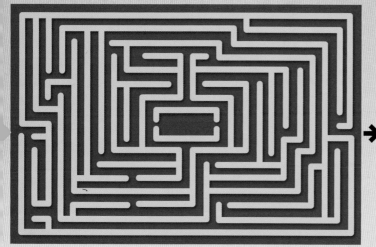

To go from baffling someone else's brain to confusing your own, turn to pages 30–31.

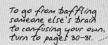

Menacing maze
The more twists and turns a maze has, the harder it is to navigate. See if you can find the route through this maze. Sticking to one side will take you back out the way you came in—to reach the dot in the center you'll have to use trial and error.

Walk down invisible stairs

This trick is an old favorite. The secret is to make your movements as smooth as possible. Making comical facial expressions adds to the spectacle.

1. Stand behind a sofa and tell your audience that there is an invisible staircase that only you can see hidden behind it.

You can use any waist-height solid object, not just a sofa.

You will need:

Hot dog

Wooden spoon

Make a friend scream

The human mind is a sensitive thing — so sensitive, in fact, that it can be made to feel pain through an inanimate object. Try this trick out on an unsuspecting friend.

TOP TIP
If you don't have a hot dog at hand, a long, thin cookie is a good, but messy, alternative.

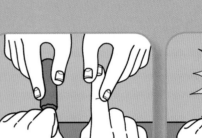

1. Have a friend put their fists at the edge of a table top, with the index finger of their right hand resting on the table. Place a hot dog where the index finger of their left hand would be. Tell your friend you're going to make them think

2. Start by gently stroking the finger and the hot dog at the same time. Blow on both the finger and the hot dog, and in a soothing voice ask if your friend can feel anything. Your friend will keep on telling you that what you're doing is having no effect.

3. Keep stroking and blowing, being gentle and soothing, and then suddenly smash the spoon down on the hot dog. Do not hit the finger. Your friend will yell out, thinking, for a moment, that their finger has been hurt.

Bodysurf at home

Bodysurfing involves riding a wave flat on your front, without a board. It takes skill and dedication to master. Round up a few friends to put this easier (and drier) version to the test.

1. Recruit four of your friends and get them to lie down on their stomachs, as close together as possible. Lie down on your stomach across their backs, with your arms stretched out in front of you.

2. Ask your friends to roll their bodies at the same time and in the same direction. See how long you can "surf" without falling off!

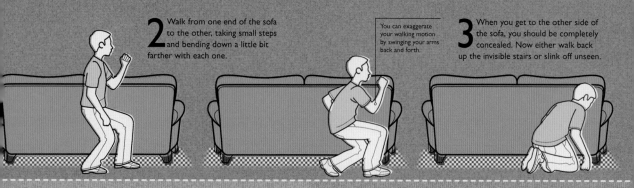

2 Walk from one end of the sofa to the other, taking small steps and bending down a little bit farther with each one.

You can exaggerate your walking motion by swinging your arms back and forth.

3 When you get to the other side of the sofa, you should be completely concealed. Now either walk back up the invisible stairs or slink off unseen.

Levitate

Levitation means hovering in the air unaided. You can create the illusion that you're defying gravity with this simple trick. Just take care not to let your audience stray from its position!

Walk through paper

If you're looking for a way to mystify your friends, tell them that you can walk through a sheet of paper and then challenge them to try it. Once they've given up, show them how it's done.

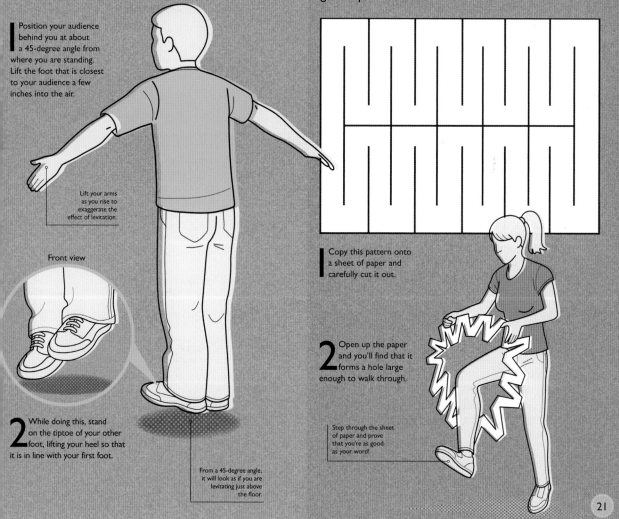

1 Position your audience behind you at about a 45-degree angle from where you are standing. Lift the foot that is closest to your audience a few inches into the air.

Lift your arms as you rise to exaggerate the effect of levitation.

Front view

2 While doing this, stand on the tiptoe of your other foot, lifting your heel so that it is in line with your first foot.

From a 45-degree angle, it will look as if you are levitating just above the floor.

1 Copy this pattern onto a sheet of paper and carefully cut it out.

2 Open up the paper and you'll find that it forms a hole large enough to walk through.

Step through the sheet of paper and prove that you're as good as your word!

21

Strum guitar chords

A guitar has six strings that get thicker and lower pitched from 1 to 6. Plucking one string produces a single note. Plucking while holding the string down above one of the frets gives a different note. Strum two or more strings together in the right combination and you are playing a chord. First learn your way around the guitar and then start strumming!

In these instructions, an X above a string indicates that you don't play it at all.

An O indicates that you should strum this string.

Holding a guitar

Hold the neck of the guitar with one hand so that the back of the instrument is flat against your body. Make sure that the guitar is the right way up—the thickest string should be on top, with the thinnest string closest to the floor.

Frets are raised bars on the neck of a guitar. The first fret is the one closest to the top of the neck, so this is the third fret.

A gray circle indicates that you need to hold your finger on the string above a fret—in this case, the second fret.

The number in the circle tells you which finger to use on the fret: 1 is your index finger, 2 is your middle finger, 3 is your ring finger, and 4 is your pinkie.

Support the neck of the guitar with the thumb of one hand so that your fingers are ready to play the frets. Strum with your other hand.

TOP TIP
Use your fingertips to press the fret and keep your fingers curled—if you touch any strings by accident, the chord won't sound right.

Chords

These are four of the simplest chords to learn, and they form the basis of many popular songs. Strum the strings from top to bottom while pressing the frets where indicated. Remember, where you see an X, don't strum the string.

To put your fingers to a different use, turn to page 185 to learn how to flick marbles

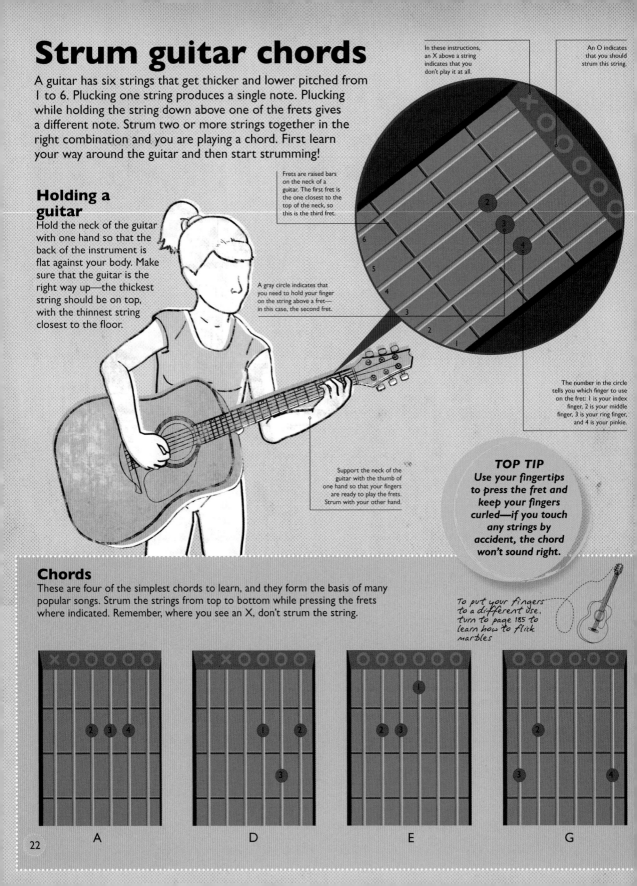

A   D   E   G

Play the blues

The 12-bar blues is a popular chord progression. This simple version uses variations of A, D, and E chords where only two strings are strummed. For each chord, you're going to strum a total of eight times. Make up your own bluesy lyrics and set your troubles to music!

TOP TIP
For a bluesy rhythm, change between the two different sounds of each chord.

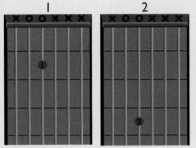
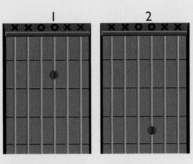
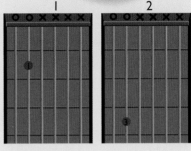

A Strum the fourth and fifth strings, playing the second fret of the fourth string (diagram 1). Strum this again. Strum the same two strings, this time playing the fourth fret of the fourth string (diagram 2). Strum this again, then repeat from the beginning.

D Strum the third and fourth strings, playing the second fret of the third string (diagram 1). Strum this again. Strum the same two strings, this time playing the fourth fret of the third string (diagram 2). Strum this again, then repeat.

E Strum the fifth and sixth strings, playing the second fret of the fifth string (diagram 1). Strum this again. Strum the same two strings, this time playing the fourth fret of the fifth string (diagram 2). Strum this again, then repeat.

A	A	A	A

Woke up this morning, | fell out of bed, | cracked my shoulder, and | split my head.

D	D	A	A

Yes, I woke up this morning, | fell out of bed, | cracked my shoulder, and | split my head.

E	D	A	E

Yes, if I'd stayed asleep, | then I wouldn't be feelin' half | dead.

Play the piano

The piano is the easiest musical instrument to get a simple tune out of. Advanced players use two hands, one to play the rhythm and the other the melody—something that's difficult or impossible to do on other instruments.

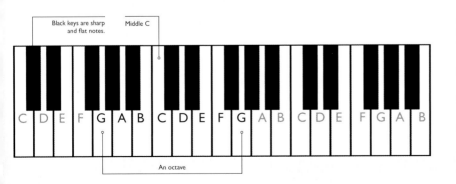

Black keys are sharp and flat notes.

Middle C

An octave

Play "Happy Birthday"

Starting with the G below middle C, hit the keys in this sequence. (The bold G means hit the G one octave higher than the one you started on.)

G	G	A	G	C	B
G	G	A	G	D	C
G	G	**G**	E	C	B	A
F	F	E	C	D	C

Move your body

Practice these moves to perfection in the privacy of your own home and your friends will be amazed when you step up to perform them on the dance floor. It goes without saying that you have to do the steps in time with the beat or it won't have the same effect.

Moonwalk like Michael Jackson

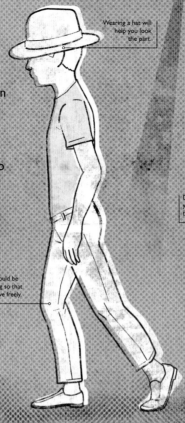

Wearing a hat will help you look the part.

Don't swing your hips—keep them straight.

Your weight should be on the other leg so that this leg can move freely.

KING OF POP
Michael Jackson made the moonwalk dance move famous when he first performed it on television in 1983.

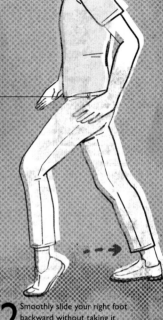

1 Stand on the ball of your left foot and put all of your weight on it, with your right foot flat on the floor.

2 Smoothly slide your right foot backward without taking it off the floor.

Do the Macarena

1 Put your right arm out in front of you, palm down. Do the same with your left arm.

2 First turn up your right palm, then your left.

3 Touch your left shoulder with your right hand, then your right shoulder with your left hand.

4 Put your right hand on the back of your head, then cover it with your left hand.

Wave the hip-hop way

1 Stretch out your arms with your fingers pointing up. Curl down the fingers of one hand.

2 Bend your elbow until it is makes a right angle, and at the same time push the heel of your hand out.

3 Straighten your arm by pushing up toward your shoulder, which should end up in a hunched position.

4 Thrust your chest out with your arms behind you and your hands pointing back.

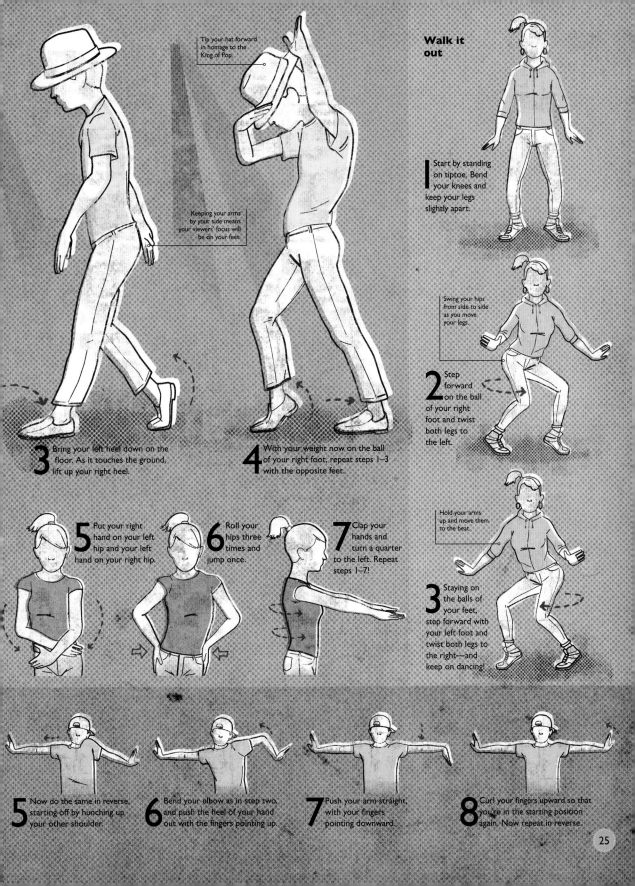

Tip your hat forward in homage to the King of Pop.

Keeping your arms by your side means your viewers' focus will be on your feet.

Walk it out

1 Start by standing on tiptoe. Bend your knees and keep your legs slightly apart.

Swing your hips from side to side as you move your legs.

2 Step forward on the ball of your right foot and twist both legs to the left.

3 Bring your left heel down on the floor. As it touches the ground, lift up your right heel.

4 With your weight now on the ball of your right foot, repeat steps 1–3 with the opposite feet.

Hold your arms up and move them to the beat.

3 Staying on the balls of your feet, step forward with your left foot and twist both legs to the right—and keep on dancing!

5 Put your right hand on your left hip and your left hand on your right hip.

6 Roll your hips three times and jump once.

7 Clap your hands and turn a quarter to the left. Repeat steps 1–7!

5 Now do the same in reverse, starting off by hunching up your other shoulder.

6 Bend your elbow as in step two, and push the heel of your hand out with the fingers pointing up.

7 Push your arm straight, with your fingers pointing downward.

8 Curl your fingers upward so that you're in the starting position again. Now repeat in reverse.

Have fun with astrology

The day of your birth indicates your star sign and, astrologists say, your personality. Do you know what your zodiac sign is—and does the description of its characteristics ring true?

The zodiac
During one year, the Sun appears to pass through 12 different constellations. This circle of star groups makes up the zodiac.

Classical elements
Astrologers split star signs into earth, fire, air, and water signs. The signs within a group all have similar characteristics.

Earth signs
You may need security and take awhile to adapt to new situations, but you are polite and sociable.

Fire signs
Upright, bright, and strong, you risk hurting people's feelings by being too honest.

Air signs
You can be cold sometimes, but you are also interested, curious, and good at communicating.

Water signs
You are sensitive and good at reading people's characters, but you may be self-indulgent at times.

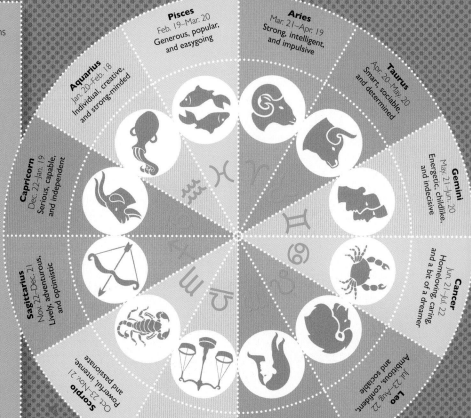

Pisces
Feb. 19–Mar. 20
Generous, popular, and easygoing

Aries
Mar. 21–Apr. 19
Strong, intelligent, and impulsive

Taurus
Apr. 20–May 20
Smart, sociable, and determined

Aquarius
Jan. 20–Feb. 18
Individual, creative, and strong-minded

Gemini
May 21–Jun. 20
Energetic, childlike, and indecisive

Capricorn
Dec. 22–Jan. 19
Serious, capable, and independent

Cancer
Jun. 21–Jul. 22
Homeloving, caring, and a bit of a dreamer

Sagittarius
Nov. 22–Dec. 21
Lively, adventurous, and optimistic

Leo
Jul. 23–Aug. 22
Ambitious, confident, and sociable

Scorpio
Oct. 23–Nov. 21
Powerful, intense, and passionate

Libra
Sept. 23–Oct. 22
Charming, gentle, and kind

Virgo
Aug. 23–Sept. 22
Creative, intelligent, and patient

Figure out your Chinese horoscope

In Chinese astrology, your animal sign is based on the year of your birth. For example, anyone born in 2000 has the dragon as their animal sign. Which animal are you?

RAT Smart, confident, funny

OX Hard working, intelligent, loyal

TIGER Fearless, strong, powerful

RABBIT Popular, kind, sincere

DRAGON Lucky, a born leader

SNAKE Smart, thoughtful, wise

1972, 1984, 1996, 2008

1973, 1985, 1997, 2009

1974, 1986, 1998, 2010

1975, 1987, 1999, 2011

1976, 1988, 2000, 2012

1977, 1989, 2001, 2013

Read palms

Turn on the gypsy charm and practice the art of palmistry—seeing what a person's hand reveals about their life.

The whole picture

Don't forget to read both hands! The marks on the dominant hand (the right hand for a right-handed person) are said to show the "public" self. The other hand reveals dreams and hopes.

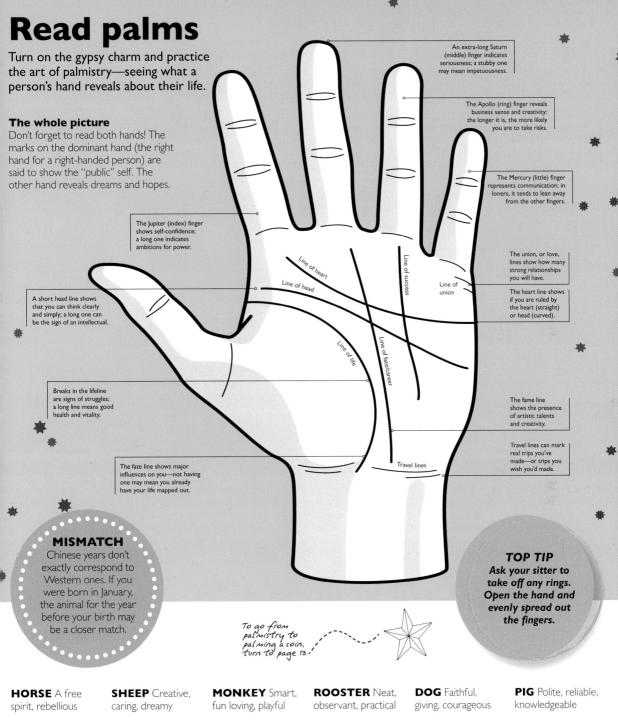

An extra-long Saturn (middle) finger indicates seriousness; a stubby one may mean impetuousness.

The Apollo (ring) finger reveals business sense and creativity: the longer it is, the more likely you are to take risks.

The Mercury (little) finger represents communication; in loners, it tends to lean away from the other fingers.

The Jupiter (index) finger shows self-confidence; a long one indicates ambitions for power.

A short head line shows that you can think clearly and simply; a long one can be the sign of an intellectual.

The union, or love, lines show how many strong relationships you will have.

The heart line shows if you are ruled by the heart (straight) or head (curved).

Breaks in the lifeline are signs of struggles; a long line means good health and vitality.

The fame line shows the presence of artistic talents and creativity.

Travel lines can mark real trips you've made—or trips you wish you'd made.

The fate line shows major influences on you—not having one may mean you already have your life mapped out.

Line of heart

Line of head

Line of success

Line of union

Line of life

Line of fate/career

Travel lines

MISMATCH
Chinese years don't exactly correspond to Western ones. If you were born in January, the animal for the year before your birth may be a closer match.

TOP TIP
Ask your sitter to take off any rings. Open the hand and evenly spread out the fingers.

To go from palmistry to palming a coin, turn to page 13.

HORSE A free spirit, rebellious

1978, 1990, 2002, 2014

SHEEP Creative, caring, dreamy

1979, 1991, 2003, 2015

MONKEY Smart, fun loving, playful

1980, 1992, 2004, 2016

ROOSTER Neat, observant, practical

1981, 1993, 2005, 2017

DOG Faithful, giving, courageous

1982, 1994, 2006, 2018

PIG Polite, reliable, knowledgeable

1983, 1995, 2007, 2019

Avoid a vampire's bite

Since the 1700s, there have been chilling reports of vampires rising from the grave to feast on the blood of the living. One bite from them and you're a bloodsucker, too. So how can you keep them at bay? Here's how to vanquish a vampire.

Don't invite trouble
Vampires cannot pass through a doorway without an invitation, so be careful who you let over the threshold. Lock your windows, too, as vampires can climb vertical walls and often make unexpected entrances.

Take a bath
Vampires cannot cross running water, so turn on the hot water, lie back, and relax, safe in the knowledge that you can't be touched.

Eat garlic
If you've invited a vampire to dinner, cook with lots of garlic. Vampires hate the smell, and they'll opt for a quick exit rather than a big bite.

Seek experts
If all else fails, you can always either expose the vampire to direct sunlight or hold a crucifix in front of them. Driving a stake through a vampire's heart is strictly for the professionals.

BLOOD ORANGE
Slavic legend tells that even fruits and vegetables can become vampires if they are bitten by a bloodsucker!

Prepare for the afterlife

The ancient Egyptians believed that at the point of death, a person's soul (or "ka") could continue to live in the afterlife, but only if the body was preserved through a process called mummification. This meant the soul could travel to the afterlife. Here's how to prepare for the trip.

Pack personal items
You'll need to take furniture, clothes, food, and drinks with you into the afterlife, so pack your tomb well. Also take any precious things you're especially fond of—jewelry, toys, even pets!

Choose an established embalmer
Look around for the best embalmer. Your embalmer will wear a jackal mask to represent Anubis, the mummification god. Your organs will be removed and your brain hooked out of your nose, but you won't feel a thing!

Flashlight

Camera

Tape recorder

Notepad and pen

Hold a ghost hunt

Staging a spookathon is the best way to lift the spirits.
A creepy location, some basic equipment, a bit of
belief, and a lot of patience are all you need.
Remember your manners when asking
apparitions to make an appearance.
Don't forget, ghosts were
once just like you!

Safety!
Never go out alone at
night, or without
telling an adult where
you've gone.

Ghost hunters recommend
checking out old houses, castles,
and graveyards because the
long and sometimes turbulent
histories can entice ghosts.

Allow plenty of time to
set up your equipment
before the hunt. Avoid
unnecessarily touching
anything at the location
to ensure the environment
is as natural as possible.

Torches and candles are
essential on the hunt to light
your way through the spooky
setting. Don't forget to bring
some spare batteries as well.

Whether you notice an
unexplained sound, a change
in temperature, or a strange
apparition, try to capture it
all on film or sound recording.

When you are ready, call
on the ghosts to appear.
Remain respectful and calm
so the ghosts do not feel
threatened, and stay alert
for supernatural signs.

Make some magical amulets
Packed with powers, magical amulets will
protect you on your journey to the afterlife.
Create your own by decorating stones.
Give them to your embalmer to insert
between the wrappings of your bandages.

Make a mask
For the finishing touch, the
Egyptians placed a funeral mask
over the mummy's head. Your
mask must resemble you and
should be made of wood,
cartonnage (similar to
papier-mâché), or gold!
Masks can be as ornate and
colorful as you choose.

...ck your body

...experiments show, your body can sometimes be ...to subconciously doing something, even when your mind is consciously telling it to do something else.

TOP TIP
The more you relax and let your brain act subconsciously, the better these tricks will work.

Arms down

At times your brain can be overprotective, stopping you from doing something even when there's no chance of you harming yourself.

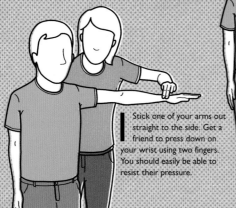

1 Stick one of your arms out straight to the side. Get a friend to press down on your wrist using two fingers. You should easily be able to resist their pressure.

2 Now try the same thing again, but this time place one of your feet (the one on the same side as your raised arm) on a small step or a pile of books.

3 Your friend will now easily be able to push your arm down. Your brain thinks your spine has become vulnerable, so it stops focusing on your arm to protect it.

Arms up

Follow these steps and it will seem as if your arms have a mind of their own, acting independently of your brain.

1 Stand in an open doorway with your arms at your side. Lift your arms out sideways and push them against the sides of the door frame. Keep pushing as hard as you can for one minute.

2 Drop your arms and relax. After a few moments, your arms should begin to rise up, as if they are floating. All that pushing caused tension in your muscles, which is why they continue to lift.

Create a force field

By exerting your muscles in certain ways, your body can be made to feel all sorts of mysterious sensations.

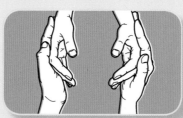

1 Put your hands out in front of you. Get a friend to place their hands on both sides of yours. Now get them to try to push your hands together as you try to pull them apart.

2 Keep doing this for 15 seconds and then stop. Relax your hands and gently bring them together. It should feel as if there is an invisible force in the way, pushing them apart.

Heavy fingers

Here, our brain tries to convince us that we can do something that seems easy but that is actually physically impossible.

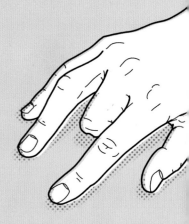

1 Lay one of your hands palmside down on a flat surface, such as a table. Tuck your middle finger under your palm so that the second joint of your finger is lying flat.

2 Try to lift your third finger. You'd think this would be easy, but because your second and third fingers share a tendon, no matter how hard you try, it won't budge.

Confuse your brain

Just as your mind can play tricks on your body, your body can play tricks on your mind, making it believe in things that aren't really happening.

Fall through the floor

Your body's senses tell your brain what's going on in the world so that your brain can tell it what to do. Sometimes, however, these messages can get a little confused.

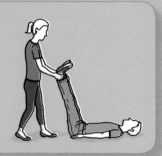

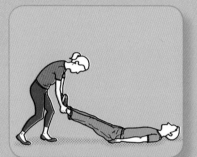

1. Lie flat on your back and close your eyes. Lift your legs up into the air and ask a friend to hold them there for two minutes. Try to stay relaxed while doing this.

2. With your eyes closed, get your friend to lower your legs back down to the floor. Stay relaxed, and after a few moments, your legs should feel as if they are dropping through the floor.

Mind over matter

Our brains are always trying to protect our bodies from doing dangerous things—and what could be more dangerous than lying on hundreds of sharp nails? Amazingly, as long as there are enough nails and you lie completely flat, evenly distributing your weight, it is possible for someone who knows what they are doing to lie on a bed of nails without causing an injury.

Get mixed up

Your brain can do many amazing things. It can solve complicated calculations, learn languages, and play fiendishly difficult computer games. But sometimes it finds it almost impossible to do two simple things at the same time.

1. Sit on a chair and stretch your right leg out in front of you. Rotate your foot around in a clockwise direction a few times until you get into a rhythm.

2. Keep rotating your foot and with your right hand try to draw a counterclockwise circle in the air. Most people find it impossible.

The Pinocchio effect

Sometimes removing just one of your senses can confuse the others. Follow these steps to see what it feels like to have your nose grow as long as Pinocchio's.

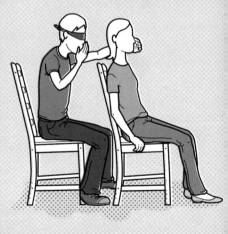

1. Sit in a chair and get a friend to sit in another chair right in front of you. Put on a blindfold and carefully place your left hand on your friend's nose and your right hand on your own nose.

2. Gently stroke the end of your friend's nose with your left hand. Do exactly the same thing to your nose. After a few moments, your friend's nose should start to feel as if it's yours.

Puzzle your eyes and brain

The optical illusions on these pages play tricks on your eyes and brain. Still images seem to move or change, dots appear from nowhere, and lines play with your perception of sizes and angles. No one knows exactly why some of these illusions work, but they'll make you cross-eyed!

Bigger or smaller?
The red line at the top appears longer than the one at the bottom, but, in fact, they are exactly the same size. This effect is caused by the black lines creating a sense of perspective.

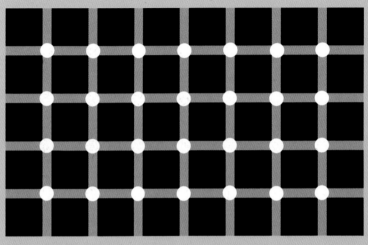

Seeing spots
If you stare at this scintillating grid, you'll see dark spots flash (scintillate) at the intersections between the squares. The effect is reduced if you tilt your head to the side or move closer or farther away from the image.

OPTICAL ILLUSIONS

Your eyes turn patterns of light and shade into electronic signals that are processed by the brain, allowing us to see the world. Information stored in your memory helps you make sense of what you see. But it can also confuse you by applying the wrong set of rules, and this creates optical illusions.

See impossible shapes

Sometimes your brain tries to see the impossible. It is possible to draw 2-D objects that appear 3-D, although they could not exist in reality. See what you make of these impossible objects.

Elliptical band
At first glance, this object appears to be a normal loop. However, if you follow the edges, you see that it is not possible for this to exist in 3-D. Try covering up either half of the image with your hand, and it looks like a normal loop.

Tricky triangle
The Penrose triangle was first conceived by English mathematician Roger Penrose. The three straight beams of the triangle appear in front and behind one another at the same time and meet at right angles to one another.

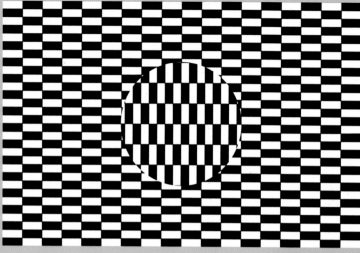

Ouchi illusion

If you move your eyes around this image, the circle in the middle appears separate from the rectangular background. It is thought that the illusion comes from the brain being unsure of where the circle ends if you are not looking directly at it.

Rotating rings

If you glance at the image below, it seems as if the rings are rotating. However, if you concentrate on just one specific area of the image, the movement appears to stop.

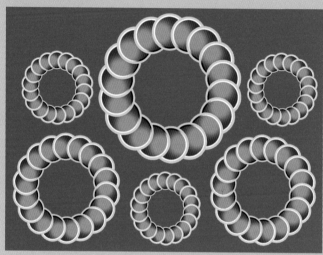

Crossed lines

Look at these four vertical lines. They appear tilted, when in fact they are perfectly straight. This illusion was created by German astrophysicist Johann Karl Friedrich Zöllner.

Find your blind spot

The place where the optic nerve (linking your eye to your brain) leaves the eye cannot detect light and is called a blind spot. The brain tries to invent information to fill in the gap. Discover your blind spot with this exercise.

1 Hold this book out in front of you at arm's length. Cover your right eye with your right hand and focus on the cross to the right of the wheel.

2 Slowly bring the book toward you while staying focused on the cross. You should gradually see the circle in the center disappear.

3 The place where your optic nerve leaves the eye cannot detect light, so your brain has filled in the gaps with the spokes of the wheel.

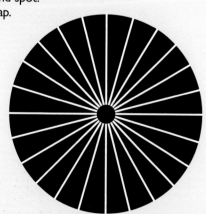

You will need:

Talcum powder

Dark paper

Soft paintbrush

Clear tape

Ink pad

Lift fingerprints

Fingertips have ridges that help detect the texture of surfaces. Thanks to the oils on your skin, you leave prints of these ridged patterns on everything you touch. Although there are four types of fingerprints, no two people have exactly the same prints. This makes them very useful for solving crimes.

1 Inspect a crime scene for a place to find fingerprints. Doors, windows, cups, and bottles are all places where people are likely to have put their hands. Remember that the prints may be invisible.

2 Dip your brush in powder and tap the handle to remove any excess. Lightly brush the powder over the surface you think may have prints on it.

3 If you find a good, clear print, apply a piece of tape to the print. Make sure it makes good contact, with no creases.

4 In one swift motion, pull the tape from the surface. It should lift the print away, too. Apply the tape to a sheet of dark paper.

5 To match the print, take fingerprints from any suspects using an ink pad. Compare the prints with the one you lifted earlier.

FINGERPRINT TYPES

Arches
This is the rarest type of fingerprint. Only about five percent of people have arch prints.

Whorls
These fingerprints look very distinctive. About 25 percent of fingerprint patterns are whorls.

Loops
Loops are the most common type of pattern. About 60–70 percent of all fingerprints are loops.

Combination
Also known as a composite pattern, these prints share characteristics of the other fingerprint types.

Read body language

We all have a variety of body postures that say a lot about how we are feeling. Some are obvious, like jumping for joy, but many are more difficult to define. There are some people who can detect the subtle gestures, but this is a real skill. Here are a few to look out for.

Hands behind head
An expression of confidence or superiority.

Crossed arms
Indicates a person is putting up a defensive barrier.

Tilted head
Usually suggests a person is bored or lost in thought.

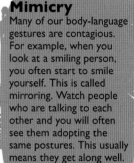

Mimicry
Many of our body-language gestures are contagious. For example, when you look at a smiling person, you often start to smile yourself. This is called mirroring. Watch people who are talking to each other and you will often see them adopting the same postures. This usually means they get along well.

Hands on hips
Often indicates impatience or possibly even anger.

Eyes looking upward
A sign of someone trying to dominate a conversation.

Looking at your lips
A strong sign of romantic attachment or intent.

Detect lies

Your emotions tend to trigger certain reactions when you are trying to deceive someone, especially if the deception is very important. You can use these body language indicators to see if someone is lying to you.

Blinking
Excessive blinking is a well-known sign of a lie.

Avoiding eye contact
As our eyes are so revealing, hiding them is suspicious.

Dilated pupils
This can occur when people experience strong emotions.

HOW LIE DETECTORS WORK

Crime investigators interrogating suspects sometimes monitor their more physical reactions using lie detectors. An increase in heart rate, breathing, or sweating in response to a certain question may show that the answer is a lie. But since habitual liars such as conmen are capable of masking their emotions when lying, lie detectors are not foolproof.

Holding body rigid
Becoming uncomfortable is common when lying.

Adjusting clothing
Deceit is often indicated by fidgeting or nervousness.

Shrugging
A liar will often feign ignorance when questioned.

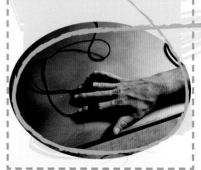

Ride a unicycle

If you can ride a bike, you can learn how to ride a unicycle. It will take time to become skilled, but you can get started with the help of two friends. You'll probably be trying this on someone else's unicycle anyway, so get him or her to help out.

1 Position the unicycle with the saddle between your legs and the wheel in front. Use your friends to steady you as you put your foot onto the closest pedal and push back a bit so that the wheel is beneath you.

2 With your arms around your friends' shoulders, sit up straight. Make sure your weight is on the seat, not the pedals. Gently push the pedals back and forth to get the feel of them, then rotate them until they are level.

3 Slowly pedal a half turn and stop with the pedals level. Do this again. Try a full turn, then two turns, always ending with the pedals level. Look straight ahead, not at the ground.

4 Keep practicing, and when you feel a little more confident, switch to holding your friends less tightly. Try to pedal some more half turns and complete turns.

5 Try steadying yourself with only one friend. See how it goes. Then briefly let go altogether—but ask your friends to stay close. Don't try to stay still; you need to keep moving to stay steady.

6 If you start feeling discouraged, take a break. To get off, lean forward and put your feet down. When you've been practicing for about an hour, you should know whether or not you will ever master this!

Rope

Trees

Weights

Some assistants

Walk a tightrope

It takes a lot of practice before you can walk a high wire over a canyon, but everyone has to start somewhere. With a slack rope set up just above the ground, you can learn the technique and simply step off when it all goes wrong!

1 Tie your rope between two trees so that it is slightly slack. Step on it and make sure that it is not more than 12 in (30 cm) from the ground.

2 Pick up a weight in each hand and get your friends to help you up onto the rope somewhere near the middle, holding your arms out straight.

3 Stand with your feet slightly across the rope. Start by standing on one leg. It's easier than standing on two because you can use the other leg to help stay balanced.

4 Try to balance with both feet on the rope. Don't look at your feet. Look forward and use your hips to keep your balance. Keep your weight on your back leg.

5 When you are able to stand without wobbling too much, take a step, find your footing, stand again, and then take another step. Keep your arms out.

6 To turn, place your back foot at a right angle and transfer your weight onto it. Swivel on the ball of your front foot and shift your weight as you face the other way.

HAUTE CUISINE
In the 1850s, French acrobat Charles Blondin became world famous for cooking an omelet on a high wire stretched across Niagara Falls.

7 When you can do all of this with some confidence, tighten and raise the rope a little. You'll be joining the circus before you know it!

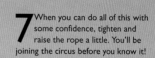

Find out how to tie a rope with the right knot on pages 148–149.

Land an airplane

Becoming a pilot requires a lot of training. However, most small noncommercial aircraft are fairly easy to control, and since they fly quite slowly, you stand a good chance of making a safe landing if the pilot should suddenly collapse. Read the instructions below in case one day you find yourself at the controls. If you have a computer with a flight simulator game, you can practice on that.

The attitude indicator, or artificial horizon, consists of a mobile picture of the horizon that moves relative to lines that represent the plane's wings.

The dial that revolves around a small image of a plane is called the heading and is a compass to help with navigation.

Air speed is measured in knots—nautical miles per hour. Anything under 70 knots in the air is dangerously slow. The green sector on the air-speed indicator represents the safe zone.

An airplane's steering wheel is called the yoke. It controls both turning (left and right) and pitch (up and down). Pull back gently to bring the nose up; push forward slightly to point it down.

1 Sit in the copilot's seat and buckle up. If the plane has only one seat, you will have to move the pilot. Take the yoke and gently pull it back until the wings on the attitude indicator (above) are level with the artificial horizon.

2 The plane is designed to be stable, so once it is level, it should fly itself. However, look for a button labeled autopilot, auto flight, AFS, or AP. Turn it on, then use the radio to call for help.

3 If you are not near an airport, you will need a reasonably flat space to land on. Look around for a big flat area such as a field. Make sure there are no overhead wires or other obstructions.

4 Begin the descent by pulling back on the throttle. Make sure the air-speed indicator stays in the green zone above 70 knots. Adjust the yoke so that the nose is about 4 in (10 cm) below the horizon.

The altimeter is one of the most important instruments and indicates altitude above sea level in meters and feet.

The throttle controls the engine. Pushing it speeds up the plane and makes it ascend. Pulling it back slows the plane and makes it descend.

TOP TIP
Don't worry about fuel. If the pilot has followed regulations, you will have enough left to land.

Get radio help

1 Put on the radio headset if there is one and use the radio to call for help. It should already be turned on. Press and hold the button to talk.

2 Say, "Mayday! Mayday!" State your plane call numbers, which should be printed on the instrument panel. Explain your situation and say, "Over." Release the button and wait for a response.

3 If you get no reply, try again on the International Air Distress channel—121.5 MHz. You should be able to find this on the radio.

4 The person on the other end should be able to talk you through the correct landing procedures. Carefully follow their instructions.

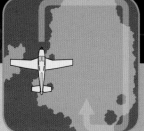

5 When the altimeter reads 1,000 ft (300 m), your landing area should be just off the right wingtip. Level out the plane and check for obstructions. If it looks clear, fly in a rectangle and make a second approach.

6 As you approach the landing zone, reduce power again but do not let the nose drop more than 3 in (8 cm) below the horizon. The plane should be 100 ft (30 m) off the ground when you come in to land.

7 You want the plane to be at just about stall speed (70 knots) when the wheels touch the ground. Gently pull back on the yoke to lift the nose a little as the plane touches down. Pull all the way back on the throttle.

8 Ignore the yoke and use the pedals by your feet. The lower pedals steer the plane and the upper brake pedals reduce your speed. Once the plane stops moving, get out and call for medical help for the pilot.

FOOD, GLORIOUS FOOD

Food is the way to most people's hearts. Who can resist the smell of a freshly baked pizza, or warm brownies, fresh from the oven? Cooking is also an essential skill for life, so discover how to have fun with food—grow your own food, make some simple, mouthwatering recipes, and then why not invite some friends over to share them with you?

You will need:

1 cup warm water

½ oz (15 g) fresh yeast

1 teaspoon superfine sugar

4 cups strong white bread flour

2 teaspoons salt

1 tablespoon olive oil

1 egg, beaten

Bake fresh bread

You'll find bread in every country of the world, though it might be flat, round, square, braided, soft, hard, sweet, savory, or sour. This recipe makes a light, white bread, that you can shape into one big loaf or into several smaller rolls, as below.

TOP TIP
If you don't have fresh yeast, you can use 0.3 oz (7 g) of dried yeast instead. Skip step 1, and in step 2 stir in the dried yeast and 1 teaspoon of sugar.

1 In a small dish, mix 3 tablespoons of warm water with the yeast and sugar. Leave in a warm place for ten minutes, until you see bubbles.

2 Sift the flour and salt into a large bowl and stir in the yeast mixture. Add the oil and enough water to make a soft dough.

TOP TIP
To knead, hold the dough with one hand and then push half of it away with the heel of your other. Lift this piece back over and press down. Turn and repeat.

3 Lightly flour your hands and the work surface and then knead the dough (see tip, left). Do this for about ten minutes, until the dough is smooth and elastic.

4 Shape the dough into a ball and place in a large oiled bowl. Cover with oiled plastic wrap and leave in a warm place for at least an hour, or until doubled in size.

5 Heat the oven to 425°F (220°C). Press your knuckles into the dough to push out the air and flatten it. Then knead lightly and divide into eight pieces. Shape each piece into a ball.

6 Place the balls of dough on an oiled cookie sheet, cover with plastic wrap, and leave to rise in a warm place for about 30 minutes until doubled in size. Brush with beaten egg and put in the oven.

7 Bake the rolls for 20–25 minutes until golden brown. If they are cooked, they should sound hollow when you tap the base.

You will need:

1 quantity of bread dough (see recipe opposite)

Olive oil for greasing

For the topping:

1 cup tomato passata (sieved tomatoes)

8 oz (225 g) mozarella cheese

1 teaspoon dried oregano

Fresh basil leaves

Salt and pepper

Cook a tasty pizza

If you are craving something savory, you can turn bread dough into delicious pizza. This recipe makes enough for four pizzas. Start by following the bread recipe opposite and go to step 4.

TOP TIP
For toppings, use your favorite ingredients—olives, ham, tuna, and salami are all delicious.

1 Preheat the oven to 425°F (220°C). On a lightly floured work surface, punch the air out of the dough, divide into four pieces and roll them into circles.

2 Place the pizza bases onto a lightly greased baking tray. Spread each one with tomato sauce, but don't go right up to the edges.

3 Scatter mozzarella over the tomato sauce, add oregano and basil, and season with salt and pepper. Bake for about 15 minutes, or until the base is crisp.

You will need:

4 ½ cups self-rising flour

½ teaspoon salt

7 fl oz (200 ml) skim milk

2 tablespoons melted butter

1 egg

Rustle up some damper

Cook this simple yeast-free bread over a campfire. It's called damper and was dreamed up by the Australian cattlemen working in the bush. This is a recipe for a luxury damper. If you're planning on cooking it out in the wild, make a simpler dough with just flour, water, and a pinch of salt.

Find out how to make a roaring campfire on pages 146–147.

4 Hold the stick over the embers of a fire and turn to brown it all over. The damper will slide off when it's cooked and will be very hot.

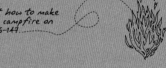

1 Put the flour and salt in a bowl and pour in the milk, butter, and egg. Mix with your hands to form a soft dough.

2 Shape the dough into a ball and pull off lumps about the size of a tennis ball. Roll into long, thin sausage shapes.

3 Wind each sausage of dough around a clean stick. Leave gaps between the coils as the dough will puff up.

1 cup all-purpose flour

Pinch salt

1 egg

1¼ cups milk

Sunflower oil for greasing

Flip a crepe

You'll find pancakes of all shapes and sizes in every country of the world. These pancakes are thin and flat, and you'll need to flip them to cook both sides. Start out by flipping them with a spatula, keeping them low. The professionals toss crepes high up in the air!

Decorate some eggs for Easter on pages 74–75.

1 Put the flour and salt in a large bowl and make a well in the center. Add the egg and about half the milk.

2 Whisk the mixture to form a thick, smooth batter. Add the rest of the milk and then whisk again.

3 Lightly oil a nonstick frying pan and place over a medium heat. Pour in 3 tablespoons of batter and tilt the pan to cover the base.

4 Cook for about a minute, or until the underside of the crepe is golden brown. Then, using a spatula, quickly flip the crepe and cook for another minute.

5 Continue with the rest of the batter until it is all used up and there are crepes for everyone. Serve with a squeeze of lemon juice and a sprinkling of sugar.

Pancake race

In many Christian countries, pancakes are eaten at the start of Lent. The tradition began in 1444 in Olney, England. A housewife was busy cooking pancakes when the bells rang, calling people to church, and she ran out still carrying her pan. A pancake race is held in Olney every year. To win, competitors must toss their pancake three times as they run.

TOP TIP
These crepes can be eaten sweet or savory. Try filling them with ham and grated cheese.

You will need:

1 ¼ cups all-purpose flour

1 teaspoon baking powder

3 pinches salt

2 tablespoons superfine sugar

1 egg

⅔ cup milk

2 tablespoons butter

1 cup blueberries

Fry up some hotcakes

These small, light, puffy pancakes are popular for breakfast and are usually, eaten with maple syrup. This recipe makes about ten pancakes.

1 Sift the flour, baking powder, and salt into a bowl and stir in the sugar. Put to one side.

2 In another bowl, or a pitcher if you have one, crack the egg, add the milk, and whisk together.

3 Pour a little of the milk and egg mixture into the flour and beat with a wooden spoon until smooth. Then gradually add the rest of the liquid.

4 Over medium heat, melt a pat of the butter in a large nonstick frying pan. When hot, ladle a spoonful of the mixture into the pan.

5 Fry for two minutes, or until bubbles appear on top and the bottom is cooked. Then flip over and cook the other side for a further two minutes.

6 Continue with the rest of the mixture. These pancakes are delicious served with fruit, such as berries or bananas, and maple syrup or Greek yogurt.

Celebrate a festival

All over the world, people love to get together to celebrate special occasions, and most are marked with food. Here are a few festivals and the food that helps mark them:

Thanksgiving

This celebration gives thanks for the survival of the early settlers in the U.S. following a harsh winter. Dinner is roast turkey, with pumpkin pie for dessert.

Day of the Dead

On November 1, Mexican families celebrate the souls of the dead who return to the land of the living for one night. Sugar skulls are decorated with the names of the deceased.

Eid al-Fitr

This Muslim festival marks the end of Ramadan, the Islamic holy month of fasting. Celebrations last for three days, and many special sweets are eaten.

Easter

This Christian festival is to celebrate the resurrection of Jesus three days after his death. People attend church and exchange Easter eggs, often made of chocolate.

Dragon boat festival

A festival celebrated across East Asia. People row boats with dragon-headed prows and drop packages of rice into the water to celebrate the life of Chinese official Qu Yuan.

Passover

The seven-day Jewish celebration to remember when Moses led the Israelites from slavery in Egypt. A special meal called Seder is eaten. Each part of the meal has a symbolic meaning.

Know your pasta

In Italy, pasta comes in many different shapes—some say as many as 600! There are thin strands for eating with light sauces, chunkier shapes to go with rich, creamy sauces, and tubes that can be stuffed with delicious fillings. Here are the names of some of the more common types.

Campanelle
(little bells)

Rotelle
(cart wheels)

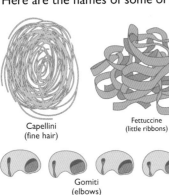

Capellini
(fine hair)

Fettuccine
(little ribbons)

Vermicelli
(little worms)

Conchiglie
(shells)

Orecchiette
(little ears)

Gomiti
(elbows)

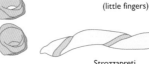

Cannelloni
(big pipes)

Radiatori
(radiators)

Penne
(quills)

Anelli
(rings)

Ditalini
(little fingers)

Fusilli
(rifles)

Farfalle
(butterflies)

Manicotti
(sleeves)

Tortellini
(little turtles)

Strozzapreti
(priest stranglers)

Cook perfect pasta

The trick for getting pasta just right is to cook it al dente, Italian for "to the tooth." This means you need to take a piece and bite it. You don't want the pasta undercooked—hard with a white uncooked middle—but it should still be springy and chewy, so keep checking.

1 Fill a large pan two thirds full of water and bring to the boil. Add a pinch of salt, then the pasta, all at once.

2 Stir immediately so that the pasta doesn't stick to the bottom of the pan, and stir from time to time so that it cooks evenly.

3 A little before the cooking time given on the package, test to see if the pasta is al dente. It should be tender but still firm.

4 Drain the pasta right away into a colander in the sink. Then shake gently to get rid of any excess water.

Make tomato sauce

One of the simplest and tastiest ways to eat pasta is with tomato sauce, a sprinkling of cheese, and some fragrant leaves of fresh basil. This quick and easy recipe makes enough for four people.

You will need:

3 tablespoons olive oil

1 carrot, peeled and finely chopped

1 onion, peeled and finely chopped

1 stalk celery, finely chopped

1 tablespoon finely chopped fresh parsley

14 oz (400 g) can chopped tomatoes

Salt and pepper

Fresh basil and grated Parmesan cheese to serve

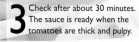

TOP TIP
You can jazz up this basic sauce by adding other ingredients such as tuna, olives, or mushrooms—whatever you like!

1 Heat the oil in a pan and gently fry the carrot, onion, celery, and parsley until soft and transparent.

2 Stir in the tomatoes, then season with salt and pepper, cover, and leave to simmer on a gentle heat.

3 Check after about 30 minutes. The sauce is ready when the tomatoes are thick and pulpy.

4 Spoon the sauce over freshly cooked pasta and serve with Parmesan cheese and fresh basil leaves.

Eat spaghetti like an Italian

Eating the long, slippery strands of this classic pasta can be a challenge, with spaghetti falling off the fork faster than you can get it into your mouth. Once you know the Italian technique, however, the days of embarrassing pasta eating are behind you.

Find out how many calories your body burns while you're asleep on pages 60–61

1 Take a fork to a tasty dish of hot spaghetti and pick up several strands of pasta between the tines (prongs) of the fork.

2 Raise the spaghetti-laden fork until the strands of pasta are clear of the dish, and twist slightly to make sure they are held firmly.

3 Dip the fork back into the dish to touch the bottom and then turn until all of the strands are wrapped neatly around the fork.

4 Place the fork in your mouth and slide the spaghetti in. Guide in any dangling strands with the fork, or quickly suck them up. *Buon appetito!*

47

Identify an egg

Eggs are good food. They're nutritious and come perfectly packaged. Do you recognize these six different eggs laid by a variety of birds?

WATER POTS
The nomadic Bushmen of the Kalahari Desert, Namibia, use empty ostrich eggshells to store precious water.

Ostrich
Average 6 in (15 cm) long, equivalent to at least 24 hen's eggs

Goose
About 3.5 in (9 cm) long—the same as three hen's eggs

Gull
Speckled eggs popular in Scandinavia

Duck
Rich and good for cakes (use two duck eggs for three hen's)

Chicken
Eggs come in brown or white, depending on the breed of bird

Quail
Tiny eggs that are a popular delicacy all over the world

Spot a broody hen

If you want a fresh egg, you need to know the signs to look for in a chicken who's likely to lay one.

1 Look for a chicken that's sitting quietly on a nest. She may close an eye or put some hay on her back.

2 If she then gets excited, raises her tail feathers, and suddenly stands up with her feet wide apart, it's a good sign.

3 Wait and watch until she bends down, strains, and an egg plops out, usually followed by a loud, proud cackle.

You will need:

6 tablespoons olive oil

12 oz (350 g) potatoes, peeled and cut into 0.75 in (2 cm) cubes

6 eggs

Salt and pepper

Cook a Spanish omelet

This delicious potato omelet is eaten all over Spain, where it is called *tortilla de patatas*. Cut a large slice for a light lunch and eat it with some crusty bread or put it inside the bread to make a chunky sandwich.

1 Heat the olive oil in a nonstick frying pan over medium heat. Add the potatoes and cook for 20–25 minutes, stirring frequently, until they are tender.

2 While the potatoes are cooking, crack the eggs into a large bowl and beat them with a fork. Season with a little salt and pepper.

Egg

Tinfoil

Hot sunny day

Fry lunch in the Sun

You can fry an egg in the heat of the Sun alone, but it has to be a very hot day, so check the temperature before you start.

1 Check the temperature—the egg will need to reach about 95°F (35°C) to cook through, so it needs to be hot.

2 Find a hot spot to do your cooking, such as a sheltered area of sidewalk.

3 Make a "pan" out of tinfoil by turning up the edges to keep the egg in and to concentrate the Sun's rays.

4 Crack the egg into the tinfoil pan, then watch and wait. If the Sun is hot enough, it will cook in minutes.

Solar frying

Every July 4, at high noon when the Sun is at its hottest, the city of Oatman, Arizona, hosts a solar egg-frying contest. Contestants have 15 minutes to fry an egg using only the power of the Sun. Judges do allow some aids, such as mirrors or magnifying glasses, to help focus the heat onto the egg itself.

Make a naked egg

A naked egg is an egg without a shell. Make one by dissolving the eggshell in vinegar, leaving just the egg in its membrane (skin).

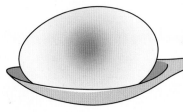

1 Put a chicken's egg in a container and cover it with white vinegar. Cover the container and put it in the fridge for 24 hours.

2 Lift out the egg, throw away the vinegar, and then put the egg back and cover with fresh vinegar. Leave for another 24 hours, then lift out the egg carefully—only the membrane will be holding it together.

5 Leave the omelet to cool for at least ten minutes, then cut into thick wedges and serve.

3 Add the egg mixture to the potatoes in the frying pan and reduce the heat to low. Leave to cook for 20–25 minutes, or until the top of the omelet begins to set.

4 Remove from the heat and slide the omelet onto a plate. Place another plate on top and turn over. Slide back into the pan and cook for five minutes.

Find out how to decorate eggs on pages 74–75.

You will need:

Oil for greasing

¾ cup butter

¾ cup superfine sugar

3 eggs

1¼ cups self-rising flour

3 tablespoons cocoa powder

½ teaspoon baking powder

For the frosting:

3½ oz (100 g) milk chocolate

3½ oz (100 g) semisweet chocolate

7 fl oz (200 ml) heavy cream

Bake a chocolate cake

There's no better way to celebrate a special occasion than with a delicious home-made chocolate cake that everyone can share. This cake is easy to make and fun to decorate. The only tricky part is trying not to eat it before your guests arrive!

1 Grease two nonstick, 20 cm (8 in) round cake pans, and line the bases with parchment paper. Cream the butter and sugar together in a bowl until fluffy, then slowly beat in the eggs.

2 Preheat the oven to 350°F (160°C). Sift the flour, cocoa powder, and baking powder into a bowl and fold them into the creamed mixture.

3 Divide the mixture equally between the two cake pans, smoothing the tops. Bake for 20–25 minutes, or until firm. Turn the cooked cakes out onto a cooling rack.

Learn how to play "Happy Birthday" on pages 22–23.

4 To make the frosting, break the semisweet and milk chocolate into a bowl and gently melt them over a pan of simmering water.

5 Remove the pan from the heat. Allow the chocolate to cool for five minutes and then stir in the cream. Leave the mixture to thicken.

6 When the cakes are completely cool, put one on a serving plate and spread one fourth of the frosting over it.

Birthday candles

A popular tradition is to decorate a birthday cake with small candles and blow them out all at once to make a secret wish come true. It's thought to have started with the ancient Greeks, who believed the smoke from the flames would carry an offering up into the sky, where the god Artemis lived.

7 Put the other cake on top and spoon over the rest of the frosting. Spread it to cover the top and the sides until the cake is evenly coated.

Sprinkle pattern

If you don't like frosting, a simple and pretty way to decorate a plain cake is with a confectioner's sugar pattern. All you need is a paper doily—and if you don't have one, you can make one.

1 Take a piece of paper large enough to cover your cake, fold in half, then quarters, and finally fold diagonally.

2 Cut the outer edge into gentle curve (if you open the paper up, you will see that it is a circle).

3 Make cuts along the edges to create a pattern. Open up to reveal your doily.

4 Sift one tablespoon of confectioner's sugar over the doily, then carefully lift it off to reveal the pattern.

***TOP TIP**
Another quick way to decorate a cake is to arrange small colorful candies in a pattern on top.*

8 Leave to set, then decorate. Small strawberries are a great fruity combination with chocolate and look pretty.

Wish a friend "Happy Birthday"

Here's how to congratulate friends all over the world when it's their birthday.

Joyeux anniversaire
French

Feliz cumpleaños
Spanish

Herzlichen glückwunsch zum geburtstag
German

Tanjobi omedeto
Japanese

Sheng ri kuai le
Chinese

Janmadina mubaraka ho
Hindi

Buon compleanno
Italian

Eed melad saeed
Arabic

Feliz aniversário
Portuguese

S dnem razhdeniya
Russian

You will need:

Cocktail ingredients
of your choice

Ice

Sugar-rimmed glass
(see box)

Cocktail shaker

Mix fabulous fruit cocktails

These delicious drinks are best shaken, not stirred! If you don't have a cocktail shaker, mix drinks in a clean plastic bottle and pour through a strainer.

TOP TIP
You can use the lid of the cocktail shaker to measure the ingredients.

Get shaking

Put the ingredients (except the carbonated ones) in a shaker with a few handfuls of crushed ice. Check that the top is on tight, then shake. Strain into an ice-filled glass and add any carbonated ingredients.

Perfect presentation
To give your glass a funky, frosted rim, dip it first in a saucer of lemon juice, then in a saucer of superfine sugar. Fruit slices, cocktail cherries, mint sprigs, paper umbrellas, and plastic monkeys all make great garnishes!

Cinderella
Shake 5 tablespoons each of orange juice and pineapple juice. Strain and mix with 8 tablespoons of lemon-flavored soda.

Bora Bora
Shake 8 tablespoons of pineapple juice, 1 tablespoon of grenadine, and a dash of lime juice. Strain and mix with 8 tablespoons of tonic water.

Serve homemade lemonade

Nothing beats the tangy taste of freshly made lemonade. If your lemons are unwaxed, you can add strips of zest for extra flavor. This recipe makes enough for about six thirst-quenching glasses.

1. Cut the lemons in half and squeeze out the juice. Pick out any seeds by hand, then pour into a pitcher. If you use a strainer, you'll lose the lemony pieces.

2. Gently heat the sugar in a pan with one third of the water, stirring constantly. When the sugar is dissolved, pour onto the lemon juice and stir.

3. Mix with the remaining water and chill in the refrigerator. When the lemonade is nice and cold, serve with ice cubes and fresh lemon slices.

Make real hot chocolate

Watch out if you try this dreamy drink—you may never be happy with powdered hot chocolate again. This quantity makes enough for one large mug.

TOP TIP
No marshmallows? Top with a squirt of whipped cream and a dusting of cocoa.

1 Break the chocolate into pieces and place in a heatproof container. Heat up the milk and pour one third of it over the chocolate. Leave for a minute.

2 Whisk the chocolate milk till smooth. Reheat the remaining milk and pour into the container with the vanilla, whisking constantly.

3 Pour the hot chocolate into your mug. Stir in a spoonful or two of sugar to taste, if you wish, then top with a layer of mini marshmallows.

Whiz up smoothies

Smoothies use whole fruit, so they're packed full of nutrients. They're also super yummy! These recipes all make one drink, but why not double the ingredients and freeze the leftover mixture in popsicle molds?

In the mix

Making smoothies is so easy. Simply whiz the ingredients in a blender or food processor, pour, and drink! Here are four cool combinations, but why not have fun inventing your own smoothie recipes?

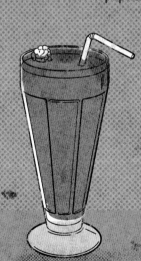

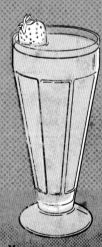

Fruity cooler
Blend a quarter of a melon, 6 oz (175 g) ripe strawberries, and 1 cup of orange juice for a really summery smoothie.

Chilly berry shake
Whiz up 1¾ cups of frozen mixed berries with ⅔ cup of whole milk for a satisfying smoothie shake.

Peach treat
Put 1 banana, 2 ripe peaches, and the juice of 2 oranges in the blender for a super-sweet anfantastically fruity smoothie.

Yummy yogurt
If you like things creamy, blend 1 banana, 6 oz (175 g) of strawberries, ½ cup of vanilla-flavored yogurt, and ½ cup milk. Yum!

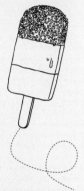

Go from ice lollies to an ice house – learn how to build an igloo on pages 134–135.

Chill fruity popsicles

Striped red, orange, and green, these refreshing popsicles look just like traffic lights. You'll need six popsicle molds and six lollipop sticks to make them. On your mark, get set, go!

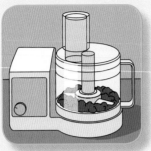

1 Wash, hull (cut off the top part), and quarter the strawberries, then blend with 1 tablespoon of sugar. Pass the purée through a strainer.

2 Spoon the strawberry purée into the bottom third of each popsicle mold. Place the molds in the freezer for an hour.

3 Pour some orange juice into each mold to make the middle layer. Return to the freezer for another hour.

4 Cut the top and bottom off each kiwi fruit, take off the skin, and chop roughly. Blend the fruit with 2 tablespoons of sugar. Again, strain to get rid of the seeds.

5 Spoon the kiwi purée into the molds. Leave space at the top, as the mixture will expand as it freezes. Freeze for another hour before serving.

Fast-freeze ice cream

Check out this amazing technique for super-fast freezing. Thanks to the not-so-secret ingredient (salt) and some smart science, you can turn a milky vanilla mix into perfect ice cream in less than ten minutes!

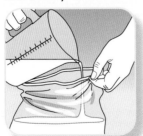

1 Pour the milk, sugar, and vanilla into a small sealable freezer bag. Squeeze out any air, zip shut, then place inside a second small sealed bag.

2 Put the ice in a large sealable freezer bag and sprinkle it with the salt. Put the bags containing the ice-cream mixture in the middle.

3 After squeezing out any air, seal the big bag. Squish its contents to chill the mixture. Wear gloves or wrap the bag in a dishtowel.

Make an ice bowl

This cool container is perfect for displaying fresh fruit or chilled treats. It's decorated with flowers and fruit, but you could use anything—how about cute plastic toys?

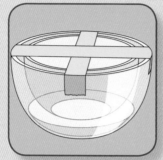

1 Fill the large bowl with 1 in (2.5 cm) of water and freeze for three hours. Put the small bowl inside the large one. Keep it centered with packing tape.

2 Pour water almost to the top of the gap between the bowls, then drop in the decorations. Use a fork to move them into position.

3 Place in the freezer for eight hours. Remove the tape and the small bowl, then turn the large bowl upside down so that the ice bowl slips out.

TOP TIP
If the ice bowl doesn't slide out right away, put the large bowl in lukewarm water for a few minutes.

4 Use your ice bowl to serve summer fruit, ice cream, sorbet, or any other dessert that is best kept chilled.

4 After five to ten minutes of squishing, your ice cream will be ready. Serve in cones—yum!

SALT AND ICE

Water freezes at 32°F (0°C), but salty water has a lower freezing point. Seawater turns to ice at around 28°F (−2°C). Salt lowers the freezing point of ice and makes it melt—that's why we use salt on icy roads in the winter. In the same way, adding salt to the crushed ice in the bag makes it melt faster. As it melts, the ice takes heat energy from its surroundings, including the ice-cream mixture, so it becomes very cold, very fast!

Beekeeper's suit and gloves

Beehive

Smoker

Long knife

Honey extractor

Extract honey

Honey is a form of sugar that honeybees make from fragrant flower nectar. Foraging bees gather the nectar and take it back to the hive, where other bees turn it into honey. Most honeybees now live in artificial beehives. Inside, the bees build their honeycombs in frames that can be lifted out once a year so that the honey can be harvested.

The variety of flowers in the area will affect the flavor of the honey.

Inside the hive

Foraging honeybees bring nectar to the hive and pass it to other bees who chew it for about half an hour to turn the sugar into a different form that lasts longer. They put this sugar in wax honeycomb cells, fan it with their wings to remove water, and seal the cells with wax. Bees use the honey as food for themselves and their young.

Safety!
Don't approach a beehive without wearing special protective clothing. If bees think you are a threat to the hive, they will sting you to protect it.

1 Dress up in a beekeeper's suit and gloves to stop any angry bees from getting at your skin and stinging you. Be careful to seal any gaps—if a bee gets trapped inside the suit, it will not be fun for you or the bee!

2 Take off the roof of the beehive and puff smoke into it with a special smoker. This makes the bees think there's a fire. They eat some honey to prepare for evacuation, and this makes them less inclined to sting you.

3 Lift off the top part of the hive, which is where the bees make their honey. Then put the hive roof back on before the bees get too angry. Carry the top section away from the hive and lift out the frames one at a time.

Check the honeycomb regularly to see how the bees are doing.

PERFECTLY PRESERVED
If it is stored in sealed jars, honey can stay edible for centuries. It doesn't decay like other foods—although very old honey may not have much flavor.

Each hive may be home to 60,000 bees, but they don't all make honey. Others make honeycomb, clean the hive, and feed the young.

4 Take each frame and carefully cut the wax capping off the honeycomb, using a long heated knife to slice through the wax. Some beekeepers use an electric heated knife. The honey will start dripping out of the comb.

5 Before you lose any honey, put each uncapped honeycomb frame into a honey extractor. This is like a metal drum with a rotating framework inside, usually powered by an electric motor. Keep adding frames until it is full.

6 When you turn on the extractor, it spins the honeycombs, forcing the honey out. The honey collects in the bottom of the extractor, which has a tap so you can drain it out. Filter to remove any wax and pour into jars. Mmmm!

Be the perfect guest

Foreign travel can be a minefield when it comes to manners. What's polite in one country might be the height of rudeness in another, so do your research on the country you are visiting. Here are a few things to watch out for.

TOP TIP
In some countries, you don't eat from your own plate, but from a big central dish. Don't reach over and grab the best pieces; always take the food in front of you.

Welcome?

Early or late?
In Austria and Latvia, lateness is disrespectful, but in Mexico, always arrive 30 minutes late.

Present problems
You may think it's a nice gesture to bring your hosts a gift, but in Iceland, it's an insult!

The imperfect gift
Never give a clock in China; it means you're counting the time until the recipient's death.

Flower power
Even a gift of flowers can go wrong—in Russia, yellow means you want to end the friendship.

Table manners

First refusal
In China, you should always refuse an offer of food at first, so as not to appear greedy.

Eat with your fingers
In many countries, eating with your fingers is commonplace, but always use your right hand.

A good burp
Don't be afraid to slurp and burp in China—it shows you're enjoying your meal.

Clean plate
If you clear your plate in Hong Kong, your generous host will keep bringing you more food.

Bad habits

No pointing
Be careful where you point; in some countries, it's very rude and a sign of anger.

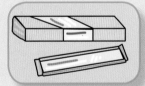

Gum-free zone
In Singapore, chewing gum is illegal. Bring gum into the country and you'll get a year in prison.

Stop sniffing
Blowing your nose in public is considered revolting in Japan, and dirty tissues are even worse.

No licking
Thais hold their king in high regard, and licking a stamp with his image is disrespectful.

Fold a napkin

If you're having friends over for a special meal, it's nice to decorate the table. For an impressive finishing touch, why not fold the napkins into regal crowns?

1 Fold a square napkin in half diagonally. Turn it so that the open ends are pointing away from you.

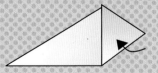

2 Fold the bottom right corner, bringing the point up to the top middle corner.

3 Bring the bottom left corner up to meet the middle corner, creating a diamond shape.

Use chopsticks

In China, Japan, South Korea, or Vietnam, most food is eaten with chopsticks, which can be tricky to use if you're not sure how to hold or handle them. But with a little practice, you'll soon be leaving a clean plate.

1 Take one chopstick and hold it so that it rests in the crook of your thumb and the top joint of your middle finger.

2 Hold the other chopstick above it, between your thumb and index finger.

3 Line up both chopsticks so that they are parallel. Practice lifting the top one while keeping the first one still.

4 Now try picking up a piece of food. Lift to your mouth and enjoy!

TOP TIP
Except in South Korea, where a spoon is used for soupy dishes, lifting a bowl to your mouth and using chopsticks to shovel in food is perfectly acceptable.

Chopstick etiquette

There are different rules for chopstick use, according to the country you're in, but here are a few key points to be aware of.

Side by side
Always place chopsticks side by side. Leaving them in a V or X shape is a bad omen in Japan and Hong Kong.

Straight up
In Asia, never stand chopsticks upright in a bowl of food—they look like funeral incense sticks.

No stabbing
Don't skewer food with your chopsticks; it's considered extremely bad manners.

Neatly press this fold.

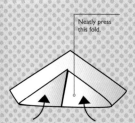

4 Turn over and fold up the bottom of the napkin diamond about halfway.

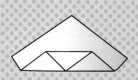

5 Fold the point down again to meet the bottom edge of the napkin. Press firmly.

The folded side of the napkin should be on the inside of the crown.

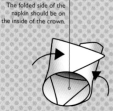

6 Curl up the ends of the napkin so that they overlap and tuck one inside the other.

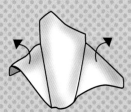

7 Turn over, stand the crown up, pull down the top corners and open them out.

Eat a balanced diet

Having a healthy diet means eating a range of foods in the right balance. The plate below shows the five main food groups and the proportion of each that you should consume over the course of one day, including drinks and snacks. Stick to these guidelines, don't skip breakfast, do drink lots of water, and you'll be well on your way to a balanced diet.

TOP TIP
Avoid processed foods, which often contain high levels of hidden sugar and salt.

Milk and dairy products
These foods contain protein, vitamins, and calcium. However, some of them, such as butter, cheese, and cream, can be very high in fat. Make sure you don't eat too much of them or try to choose lower-fat varieties.

Starchy foods
This group includes bread, rice, potatoes, and pasta and should form the basis of your meals and make up one third of your diet. These foods are a good source of energy and contain many vital nutrients, such as calcium, fiber, iron, and B vitamins. Wholegrain varieties are best because they are rich in fiber, which helps digestion.

High-fat and high-sugar foods
Fats help digestion and contain vital fatty acids, while sugar provides energy. But we need only very small amounts—eating too much leads to weight gain. Many foods in the other groups contain fats and sugars, so high-fat and high-sugar foods like chips, candy, and soda should be eaten only as a treat.

Nondairy protein
Meat, fish, eggs, beans, and lentils are all sources of protein—an essential nutrient that the body uses to make new cells and repair tissue. You don't need that much protein-rich food. Eat lean cuts of meat and remove the visible fat. Try to eat two portions of fish per week.

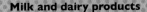

Fruit and vegetables
These foods are full of vitamins and minerals but are naturally low in fat. They should form one third of what you eat each day and you should try to eat a mixture of different fruit and vegetables to get the full range of nutrients that your body requires.

To perfect your tennis serve, turn to pages 158–159.

Count calories

The energy content in food is measured in thousands of calories (kcal). Do you know how many calories you are eating? Here are the numbers for some common snacks?

Apple
50 kcal

Banana
100 kcal

Boiled egg
75 kcal

Chicken breast
160 kcal

Slice of pizza
275 kcal

Candy bar
300 kcal

Calories
Calories aren't an ingredient but are a way of expressing how much energy there is in a food. It's possible to consume negative calories—munching on an ice cube requires more energy than the ice provides. Some foods can be low in calories but very nutritious. The key is avoiding foods that have many calories and little else.

Burn 100 calories

How many calories a person needs depends on their age and gender. A typical boy aged 11–14 needs about 2,200 kcal a day, while a girl the same age needs 1,800 kcal. If you are very active, you'll need more calories. See how far 100 calories will get you.

Running
Put your sneakers on and go for a ten minute run.

Soccer
He shoots, he scores! Play soccer for 15 minutes.

Housework
Bust that dust for 20 minutes.

GET IN SHAPE
A muscly body burns more calories than a flabby one—for every 1 lb (450 g) of muscle, the body needs an extra 50 kcal in order to function.

Cycling
Ride a bike for 15 minutes.

Tennis
Hit a ball around a court for 15 minutes.

Swimming
Practice your front crawl for 15 minutes.

Fidget
Jiggle your legs and drum your fingers for 45 minutes.

Dancing
Boogie on down for 20 minutes.

Walking
Take a brisk 30-minute stroll.

Play pool
Shoot some pool for 30 minutes.

Bowling
Knock down pins for 30 minutes.

Grow your own food

It's easy to grow your own food. You just need to buy some seeds, plant them in pots of soil, water them, and watch them grow. Even better, if you have a garden or access to a plot of land, you can use it to dig and plant. It's fun! The food you harvest will taste much better than the food you buy, because it's so fresh.

POTTING AND PLANTING

• Plant most vegetable seeds in small pots of seed compost in the early spring and place them on a sunny windowsill.

• When they sprout, put them outside during the day and bring them in at night. Leave them out for longer and longer and keep them out once any risk of frost has past. After a few weeks, you can plant them in your garden or in outdoor containers.

• Select a sunny garden site. Most vegetable crops need plenty of light. Ideally, don't plant the same crops in the same patch two years in a row. Switch them around.

• If you are planting up part of a garden plot, dig over the ground and remove any weeds, especially the ones with big, juicy roots. Then add some fertilizer or garden compost to the soil.

Potatoes

Buy seed potatoes and put them near a window to sprout in the light. Plant them in holes 6 in (15 cm) deep, 12 in (30 cm) apart. The plants will grow lush and green. When they flower, dig one up to see if the potatoes are ready.

TOP TIP
If the weather is dry, water your plants every evening. Use liquid fertilizer once a week.

Corn

Sow the seeds indoors in pots. Plant them in a "block" of at least 4 × 4 plants more than 12 in (30 cm) apart so that pollen from the flowers blows onto the other plants. Harvest the cobs when their tassels turn brown.

Pots and patios

There are many tasty things that you can grow even if you don't have a garden. You just need plenty of big pots, tubs, and troughs that you can fill with potting compost and put on a sunny patio or balcony. You can even use window boxes!

TOP FRUIT
The tomato is a fruit, not a vegetable. In fact, it's the world's most popular fruit—more than 2.5 million are eaten each day.

Tomatoes

Sow these indoors and then plant them out in big pots placed in a sunny spot. Use tall canes to support the plants as they grow and feed them with tomato fertilizer.

Lettuce leaves

Sow these directly into a big pot or hanging basket (so slugs can't get at them). As they grow, pick the young leaves and use them in salads. You can do this all summer long.

Carrots

You can plant carrot seeds directly in cultivated soil. Thinly scatter them in a strip 6 in (15 cm) wide. Cover them with another 0.5 in (1.5 cm) of soil and water them. When they sprout, thin them out. You can eat carrots when they are quite small.

Climbing beans

Sow these indoors in pots. Prepare a fertile bed of soil and put up a tepee of canes or sticks. When there is no more risk of frost, plant your beans, and they will climb up the canes. Looking good!

Discover how to make your own compost on page 100.

Squashes

These include butternut squash, zucchini, and pumpkin. Sow the seeds indoors in pots and plant a few out in very fertile soil, at least 18 in (45 cm) apart. Choose an open, sunny site with a lot of space.

Herbs

All types of herbs grow well in pots. Many also have a delicious fragrance. Try basil, thyme, oregano, mint, chives, parsley, cilantro, and tarragon. Grow a bay tree, too.

Strawberries

Put several plants in a big pot or in a strawberry tower that has planting pockets on the sides. Plant them in late summer, and they will give you a juicy crop eight months later.

Chilies

If you like hot, spicy food, try growing chili peppers. They are ideal for sunny balconies and patios. Sow the seeds indoors, plant them outside, and feed them with tomato fertilizer.

GET CREATIVE

Here are lots of ideas to get you cutting, sticking, folding, and painting. Find out how to turn paper into an origami animal, a papier-mâché bowl, a water bomb, or a piñata packed with treats. Try knitting a scarf and knotting a friendship bracelet. Or have fun with your camera and master the arts of photography and animation.

Sheet of paper

Markers

Fly a paper plane

Who hasn't folded and flown a paper airplane? There are many different designs, but this is the simplest. It flies best inside, where there are no sudden gusts of wind.

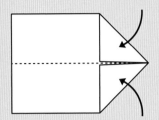

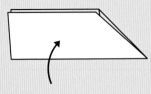

1 Fold the sheet of paper in half lengthwise to make a central crease, then unfold.

2 Fold the two end corners in to meet the crease. The point at the end is the nose of your airplane.

3 Fold the paper again along the central crease. The two folded-in edges should be hidden inside.

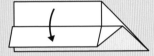

4 Fold back one edge so that it almost reaches the central fold. This will be one of your plane's wings.

5 Turn over the plane and fold back the other edge. Again, stop just short of the central crease at the bottom.

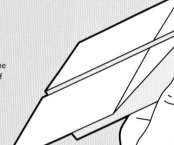

6 Holding the plane at the central crease, pull out the two wings so that they're horizontal.

7 Hold the plane between your thumb and index finger, point the nose upward, and let go!

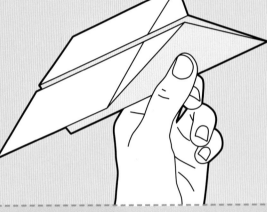

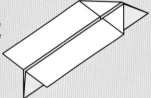

Square piece of paper

Water

Make a water bomb

Did you know that with just a square piece of ordinary paper, some water, and a bit of nimble folding you can make your very own missiles? Water bombs are every prankster's dream—for the full effect, chill the water with ice cubes first!

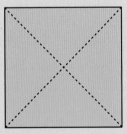

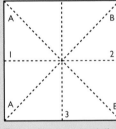

1 Fold your piece of paper in half along both diagonals. Then unfold and turn over.

2 Now fold the paper in half along both horizontals. Add small pencil labels as shown.

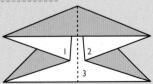

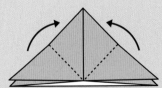

3 Fold points "1" and "2" onto "3," "A" to "A," and "B" to "B" so that the model becomes a triangle.

4 Fold the two outside points of the triangle back to reach the top.

5 Turn the model over and repeat step 4.

6 Fold the side points into the center.

7 Fold down the top edges and tuck them in.

Fold a boomerang

Boomerangs are throwing sticks that come back to the person who has thrown them. They traditionally have two "wings"—but can have three or even four.

1 Copy the basic boomerang shape shown here onto a piece of cardboard. Then cut it out.

2 Fold down the edges, as shown by the dashed lines on the template.

QUICK STICK
Boomerangs are based on the throwing sticks used by Australian Aborigines. Traditional ones are decorated with dots and swirls.

The folded-down edge will make your boomerang more aerodynamic.

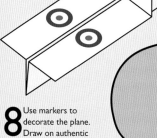

8 Use markers to decorate the plane. Draw on authentic air-force symbols (see above) or invent your own designs.

8 Turn over and repeat steps 6 and 7. Blow into the end where the loose paper is to create a cube.

9 Pour in water and then throw the bomb at your chosen victim.

Throw a boomerang

You'll need to practice, but it won't take long for you to become an expert boomerang thrower!

1 Raise the boomerang with the thin edge at the front, ready to slice through the air.

2 Swing your arm forward in a curving motion to launch the boomerang—then get ready to catch it!

See pages 72–73 for other fun things to do with paper.

Foil roasting pan
or other large
deep-sided tray

Marbling paints
or marbling inks

Paper

Lots of
old newspaper

Make marbled paper

Wrapping a present in handmade paper is the perfect way to make
it special. Marbling is a simple technique for jazzing up plain paper.
The results are always spectacular and unique.

1 Protect your work surface with old newspaper. Then pour about 1 in (2 cm) of water into the foil pan.

2 Carefully drip drops of paint or ink onto the surface of the water. Then add a few more colors.

3 Swirl the colors on the surface of the water with a pencil to make feathery patterns.

TOP TIP
*For inspiration,
visit secondhand
bookstores. Old
books often have
beautiful marbled
paper on their
inside covers.*

4 Carefully roll your sheet of paper down so that it floats on the surface of the water.

5 Now carefully roll the paper back. The marbling paint or ink lifts away onto the paper.

6 Leave your marbled paper on some old newspaper to dry, colored side up.

Rectangle of white
or light-colored
tissue paper

Paintbrushes

Colored inks

Dye tissue paper

Tissue paper protects fragile gifts—and makes a great
rustling noise as it's ripped off! Try this simple technique
for creating gorgeous patterned tissue paper.

TOP TIP
*Just use a little
bit of water. Your
colors will be
stronger, and you'll
reduce the risk of
ripping the tissue.*

1 Fold the tissue paper sheet in half, then fold it in half again three more times.

2 Use a thick brush to paint water all over the folded paper until it's damp.

3 Paint a band of ink across the middle of the paper so that it soaks in.

4 Paint the corners of the paper a different color. Let the two colors merge.

Marbling methods

With practice, you can achieve all sorts of results. Instead of using a pencil, try moving around the paint with a comb, brush, feather, or fork. For a sunburst effect, drip each new color inside the previous one.

Spots and stripes

Instead of painting the corners with the second color, you could paint on spots or stripes. Try out subtle color combinations, such as purple and blue, and then contrasting ones like green and yellow.

5 Leave the paper to dry, then unfold carefully to reveal the pattern.

6 Flick on ink spots from the bristles of a fine brush. Leave to dry again.

Print a picture

With a bit of imagination, you can use almost anything to print repeat patterns. Just dip in paint and press down on the paper—over and over again!

To make a bird, cut a body shape out of a potato, use celery segments for its tail feathers, and real feathers for its wings.

Dip string in some paint to make the central swirls of this sun, and use segments of celery to make the rays.

Sponge prints make fanastic clouds.

Broccoli prints make lovely leafy trees.

Don't throw away vegetable leftovers; put them to good use! This pine tree was made with the core of a cabbage.

To print these beautiful flowers, simply dip the head of a broccoli stalk in paint and lightly dab it on the paper.

Corrugated cardboard can be used for long grasses.

Use the edge of a pencil to print flower stems like these.

Make a piñata

Piñatas are a fun tradition from Mexico. The hollow papier-mâché models are filled with candy and small toys and are then hung up—and bashed open—at festivals, birthdays, and other special occasions. Popular piñata shapes include donkeys and six-pointed stars. This cute little owl is fluff-tastic!

How to play

Hang the piñata from something high—outdoors a tree branch is perfect. Players take turns being blindfolded and hitting the piñata with a stick until it breaks open and the treats spill out. Then it's a free-for-all!

You will need:

Large balloon

Old newspaper torn up into strips

String

Pin

Colored tissue or crepe paper and cardboard

White glue

Candy

If you liked making this, go to page 83 for more papier-mâché fun.

TOP TIP
You can make your own glue from flour and water. Heat two cups of water and one cup of flour in a pan. Keep stirring until it thickens.

1 Blow up a large balloon and tie the end with a knot. You might find this slightly easier if you tie the knot around your finger.

2 Add a little water to the glue and use it to stick strips of newspaper all over the balloon. Leave the knot sticking out.

3 Leave to dry, then repeat step 2 two more times so that the balloon has three layers of paper. Use the pin to pop the balloon.

4 You are left with a balloon-shaped papier-mâché shell. The hole at the bottom will help you cut the flap later (see step 9).

5 Cut some tissue or crepe paper into long, thin strips. Make cuts along one edge of each strip to create fringes.

6 Working from the bottom to the top, glue alternate layers of colored fringing onto the model to make the fluffy body.

7 Cut out fringed circles of colored paper for eyelashes. Cut out white and pink semicircles for the chest and glue on.

8 Cut out the eyes, beak, wings, and feet from colored cardboard and glue them on the owl. Glue paper feathers onto the wings.

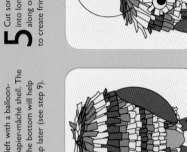

9 Cut a U-shaped flap behind the feet. Use this to fill the owl with treats, then close the flap. If the flap won't stay shut, tape it.

10 With a pencil, pierce two holes in the top. Run the string through the holes and tie the ends to make a handle.

Make origami animals

Try your hand at the ancient Japanese art of origami (paper folding). With a few nifty folds, you can transform a piece of paper into a cute creature. All of these models start with a square sheet of paper.

Fantastic fox

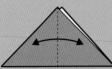
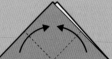

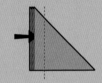

Stately swan

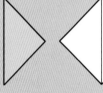

Flip over.

TOP TIP
Proper origami paper is thin and easy to fold. It has one colored side and one white side, which helps when following instructions.

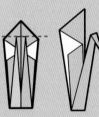
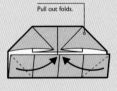

Fold in half and then pull the neck forwards.

Perky pig

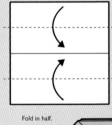
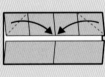

Pull out folds.

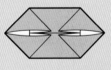
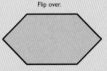

Flip over.

Fold in half.

Repeat on the other side.

Fold inward to make a nose.

Make two inward folds for the tail.

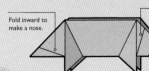
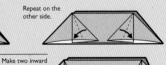
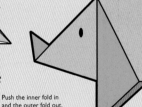
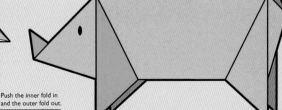

Draw an eye.

Push the inner fold in and the outer fold out.

Race a sampan

A sampan is a traditional Chinese flatbottomed boat. Make this paper version and then float it on water and watch it go.

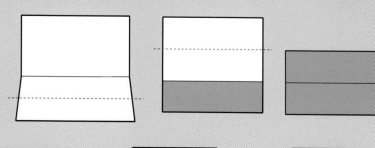

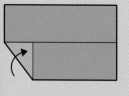 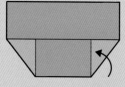 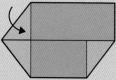 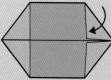

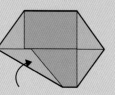 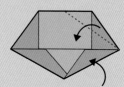 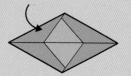 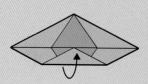

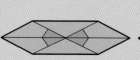 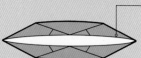 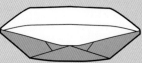

At this point, you need to turn your boat inside out. Carefully lift up one side of the central fold and push it inside out. Repeat with the other side. Be careful not to tear the paper.

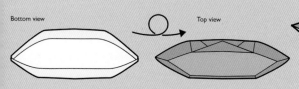 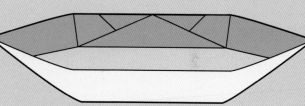

Bottom view

Top view

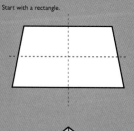

Snap a popper

This is a simple way to make a loud noise with a rectangle of paper. Raise your arm above your head and then quickly pull it down with a flick of your wrist and "bang"!

TOP TIP
Don't use origami paper to make the popper—stronger ordinary paper works best.

Start with a rectangle.

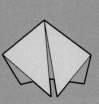

Fold in half lengthwise.

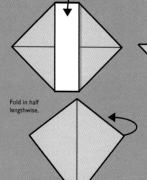 

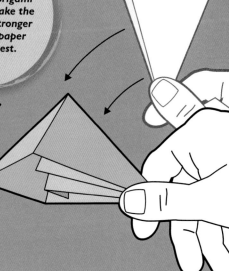

Egg

Nail   Pin

Knitting needle

Modeling clay

Decorate an egg

Eggs are a symbol of new life, so it's no wonder they are popular decorations at spring festivals, such as Easter. Use fresh eggs, but blow them first so that you can save them from one spring to the next. If you don't, they'll go off and create quite a stench.

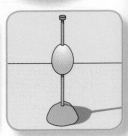

TOP TIP
Blown eggs are very fragile. Store your decorated eggs in old egg cartons so that they don't break.

1 Carefully make a pinhole in each end of the egg. Wiggle the pin until each hole is about 0.1 in (2 mm) across.

2 Now use the nail to enlarge the hole at the bottom. It should be about 0.4 in (1 cm) across.

3 Hold the egg over a bowl. Blow through the top hole to force out the yolk and white. (Save these for cooking.)

4 Stick a knitting needle through the egg and stand it in some modeling clay. Now you can decorate it.

use the insides of the eggs to make the Spanish omelet on pages 48–49.

String patterns
Dip some string in acrylic paint and then sweep it across the eggshell. When dry, repeat with different colors for a super splashy pattern.

Animal eggs
Cut shapes from felt to make animal body parts, such as ears, paws, wings, and stick them onto your egg. Use acrylic paints for the creatures' faces.

Sparkly eggs
Coat your egg in white glue, then roll it in glitter. When the glitter is set, you can glue on sparkly ribbons and colorful beads.

Vinegar

Cooking oil

Fruit and vegetables

Egg

Use natural dyes

Raid the kitchen to make some egg-cellent homemade dyes. For yellow, use a teaspoon of turmeric powder. For green, try a handful of spinach leaves. Beets create a natural red dye, onion skins make brown, and dark grapes or red cabbage make blue.

1 Half fill the saucepan with water. Add a splash of vinegar and one of the dyes. Ask an adult to boil the water for 30 minutes.

2 When the water has cooled, put in the hard-boiled eggs. Leave them till they change color, then remove and leave to dry.

3 Polish your eggs with oil to make them shine. Why not display them in a pretty straw-filled basket?

Cracking fun!
A great Easter tradition from Croatia is the *tuca*, or egg-cracking contest. Want to try? You'll need a basket of dyed hard-boiled eggs and some worthy opponents! Take an egg in your curled-up fist, with its top half sticking out between your index finger and thumb. Stay steady as your opponent hits your egg with theirs. The winner is the person whose egg stays uncracked the longest.

Egg

Acrylic paints and paintbrush

Funnel

Confetti and tissue paper

White glue

Fill some confetti eggs

In Mexico, it's traditional to throw *cascarones* (confetti-filled eggs) at Easter. They crack open on impact, showering confetti everywhere.

1 Gently tap the top of a fresh egg with a teaspoon. Break off a small circle of shell.

2 Tip the yolk and white into a bowl. Rinse the inside of the shell and pat it dry.

3 Paint the eggshell with acrylic paints. When dry, fill the egg with confetti.

4 Seal the top with tissue paper, painted over with watered-down glue.

5 Crack your colorful confetti egg over someone's head. Happy Easter!

TOP TIP
You can make your own confetti by cutting up colored tissue paper into tiny pieces.

Knot a friendship bracelet

Fashionable and inexpensive, friendship bracelets make great gifts for your best friends. The only problem is that you might want to keep them to wear yourself!

FRIENDS FOREVER
Traditionally, friendship bracelets are never taken off. They are worn until they fall apart.

1 Cut six lengths of embroidery thread in different colors. Each should be roughly the same length as your arm.

2 Line up the six threads. Knot them together about 1.5 in (4 cm) down. Separate the strands below the knot.

3 Take thread "a" and loop it over and then under and through strand "b." Holding "b," pull the knot tight. Repeat to create a double knot.

4 Now loop thread "a" over and under strand "c." Knot it and repeat again so that you have another double knot.

TOP TIP
To hold the bracelet steady while you're weaving, clip the knot to a board or safety pin it to a cushion.

5 Repeat to double knot "a" around threads "d," "e," and "f." Now thread "a" is on the far right of your row of threads.

6 Take thread "b," which is now the strand on the far left. Double knot it around threads "c," "d," "e," "f," and "a" in turn.

7 Continue, row by row, building up a bracelet of diagonal stripes. Stop when your bracelet is about the right length.

8 Knot all six strands together as you did at the beginning. Cut off the ends of the threads about 1.5 in (4 cm) below the knot.

Make a wish bracelet
Thread one pretty bead onto a short length of embroidery thread. Ask your friend to make a wish as you tie the thread around their wrist When the bracelet and bead fall off, the wish will come true!

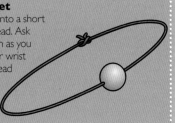

9 Place the finished bracelet around your friend's wrist. Secure the two tails with a double knot.

You will need:

2.5-ft (75-cm) length of parachute cord

10-ft (3-m) length of parachute cord

Needle and thread

Ruler

Lighter

Make a survival wristlet

This bracelet makes a great gift for a sporty friend—and it's a mini survival kit, too. It's made up of a length of super-strong cord that could save the day in an emergency.

1 Loop the shorter cord and knot it at the end. Wrap the double cord around your wrist and shorten if necessary.

2 Lie the longer piece of cord flat. Place the looped end of the short cord on top of its midpoint.

3 Bring the right-hand half of the long piece of cord around, over the top of the looped piece.

4 Take the left-hand part of the long piece over the other half. Pass it around under the loop and pull to create a knot. This is called a cobra stitch.

5 Repeat steps 3 and 4, but this time start from the left-hand side, instead of the right, to create a mirror image of the first cobra stitch.

6 With a needle and thread, secure the first stitch to the loop (shown above). Repeat steps 3, 4, and 5 to add more cobra stitches.

7 Thread the top loop through a ruler and push the knots upward so that they sit snugly together.

8 Stop about 0.4 in (1 cm) from the knot at the bottom. Trim the ends to about 0.2 in (5 mm) long.

9 Ask an adult to melt each loose end with a lighter and press it neatly into the bracelet.

Why not use parachute cord to learn how to lasso? Turn to page 149 to find out how.

TOP TIP
You can buy parachute cord from camping shops, army surplus stores, and online suppliers.

10 To fasten the bracelet, simply pass the knot through the loop!

Learn to knit

Learning to knit takes a little patience and a lot of concentration, but once you've picked it up, there are all sorts of things you can make. The easiest project is a scarf—just knit and knit until it's long enough!

Cast on

Casting on creates the first row of stitches on your needle. The first stitch is created by making a slipknot.

1 Make a loop. Take the end attached to the ball of yarn and bring a second loop through the middle of the first. Slip the second loop onto your needle and pull.

2 With the first stitch securely on the needle, take the working yarn (the yarn attached to the ball) and wrap it around your thumb from back to front.

3 Pick up the yarn from the front of your thumb with the needle, slip it from your thumb to the needle, and pull the yarn to tighten.

4 Repeat until you have the number of stitches needed. To practice the steps on this page, you need to cast on about ten stitches.

Knit stitch

There are two different methods, but this one is the easiest for beginners. Take your time and make sure you don't drop any stitches!

1 Hold the needle with the stitches on it in one hand, and take the second needle in your other hand. From the front, put the tip of the second needle through the middle of the first stitch.

2 Take the working yarn and wrap it over the second needle from back to front. The yarn will be lying in between the two needles. Hold it securely in place.

3 Now bring the second needle back the way it came, through the middle of the original stitch, taking the yarn with it. The yarn will form a loop on the second needle.

4 Slip the original stitch off the first needle, leaving your new stitch on the second needle. Repeat until you've knitted all of the stitches in the row.

Purl stitch

A purl stitch is just a knit stitch in reverse. The needle goes into the stitch from back to front, instead of front to back.

1 Push the tip of the second needle through the middle of the first stitch, but this time from behind so that the tip is pointing toward you.

2 Wrap the yarn around the second needle, from right to left. Again, the yarn will be lying in between the two needles.

3 Holding the yarn in place, pull the second needle back through the stitch on the first needle, taking the yarn with it.

4 Pull the original stitch off the first needle, leaving a new stitch on the second needle. Repeat along the row.

Bind off

When you're finished knitting, binding off secures your final row of stitches so that your work won't unravel.

1 Knit two stitches. Use your first needle (the one you are knitting from) to hook the first stitch you knitted through its middle.

2 Lift the first stitch over the second stitch, slipping the first stitch off the needle but leaving the second one on the needle.

3 Knit another stitch, so that you have got two again. As before, lift the older stitch over the newer one and off the needle.

4 Keep going until you have only one stitch left. Cut the yarn and pull the end through the loop.

create paper beads on page 82

Knit fingerless gloves

These gloves look great and will keep your hands warm when you need to keep your fingers free. Choose a bright color and decorate your gloves with buttons or beads.

You will need:

Size 7 knitting needles

1.7 oz (50g) worsted weight yarn

Embroidery needle

1 Cast on 30 stitches. The stitches shouldn't be too loose, but don't pull them too tightly either or the end of your gloves will be puckered.

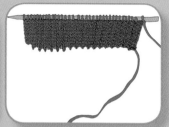

2 For the first eight rows, knit one stitch, then purl the next, alternating between knit and purl across each row. This makes a stretchy ribbed material.

3 On the ninth row, knit all the stitches, and on the tenth row, purl all the stitches. Repeat these two rows until your glove measures about 6 in (15 cm).

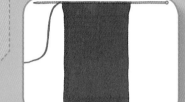

4 Repeat step two to make another eight rows of ribbing, alternating between knit stitches and purl stitches.

TOP TIP
You can knit with just about anything. Try cutting a plastic bag into strips and knit them into a quirky, hard-wearing fabric.

5 Bind off. Sew the sides together to form a tube, leaving a thumb-size hole about 2 in (5 cm) from the top. Weave in and trim any loose ends.

6 Repeat from step one to make the second glove. Carefully hand washing your gloves and leaving them to dry will make the stitches appear neater. Wear with pride!

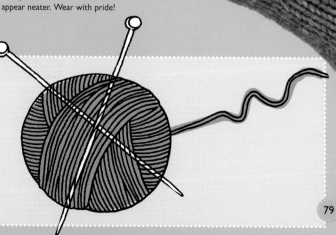

Needles and yarn
Yarn and needles come in different sizes. A chunky yarn needs a thicker needle, while a thinner yarn requires slimmer sticks. The yarn suggested above—worsted weight— is about medium thickness. It knits up quickly, so it is a good choice for a first project. You need size 7 needles—the size describes the width of the needles. Look for short needles when you're learning; they are much easier for beginners to handle.

You will need:

Garbage bags and old newspaper

White cotton T-shirt

Rubber bands or string

Spray fabric dye

Rubber gloves

Tie-dye a T-shirt

Release your inner hippie and make a terrific tie-dyed T-shirt. Start with a new T-shirt or use the technique to breathe new life into an old one—the groovy pattern will hide stubborn stains! Spray dyes are very easy to use.

1 First, protect your work surface. Cover it with garbage bags and a layer of old newspaper to stop any dye from getting through. Then lay your T-shirt out flat.

2 Pinch the T-shirt fabric to make a small bump and secure it with a rubber band. You can do both layers at once or work on the front and back separately.

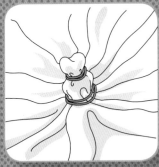

3 A single bump makes a pale ring. To make two concentric rings (one inside another), make a double bump by adding a second rubber band.

4 For a different effect, turn a single bump into a "doughnut" bump. Simply tuck the fabric at the top of the bump back through the rubber band.

5 Continue until your T-shirt is covered in different kinds of bumps. The more bumps you make, the crazier your finished design will be!

6 Before you start dyeing, read the instructions very carefully. Use sweeping strokes and always wear rubber gloves.

Tie a bandanna

The word bandanna comes from the Hindu for "tie-dyed cloth"—but any square piece of fabric will do. Once you perfect the art of tying a bandanna, you'll never have a bad hair day again. Here are four tying techniques to try.

Traditional headscarf

Fold the bandanna on the diagonal. Leaning forward, place the folded edge at your hairline. Bring the two corners around to the back of your neck and secure with a double knot.

Snug-fitting skullcap

Fold the bandanna on the diagonal, but not completely in half. Place the fold at your hairline, then doubleknot the corners and tuck the top triangle of fabric under the knot.

Top techniques

You can achieve different effects depending on how you gather and tie your T-shirts. These designs have been made using liquid dye. Always read the instructions on the packet carefully.

Deeply dotty
Tie lots of tight single bumps in your T-shirt to make a series of psychadelic circles.

Crazy circles
Start with a double bump in the middle (see step 3), then add bands below to make more rings.

Simply striped
Bunch your T-shirt up lengthways and secure rubber bands at regular intervals to make this striped effect.

Paler areas were under rubber bands, so they took little or no fabric dye.

TOP TIP
Wash your tie-dyed T-shirt on its own by hand in cold water, in case the dye runs.

7 Double-check the information on the dye, but most spray dyes are dry about half an hour after application. Undo your rubber-band bumps and your tie-dyed T-shirt is ready to wear!

Hippie headband
Fold the bandanna in half diagonally, then fold it over and over until you end up with a band about 1 in (2.5 cm) wide. Position around your head and tie at the back with a double knot.

Cowboy neckerchief
Fold the bandanna in half diagonally. Position it so that the triangle points down at the front of your neck, then tie at the back of your neck. Pull it up to cover your face—yee haw!

SCOT SPOTS
Paisley, a teardrop pattern, is popular on bandannas. Named after a Scottish textile town, it has its roots in ancient India and Persia.

Glue

Empty cereal box

Twine or ribbon

Fold a gift bag

The next time you need to wrap a present, do your part for the environment at the same time. Forget splashing out on expensive wrapping paper—turn old newspaper into a quirky gift bag instead.

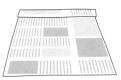

1 Take the folded edge of the paper and fold it down 1 in (2 cm) or so. Repeat and glue down (this will reinforce the top of the bag).

2 Wrap the paper around the cereal box and glue the sides together. The reinforced edge should be on the inside and at the top.

3 Remove the box. Press the paper flat, bringing the sides inward so that they crease in the middle.

4 Fold up the bottom of the bag by the same amount as its width. Firmly press and then unfold.

5 Push the sides inward, creating two flaps. Glue one flap to the other.

6 Punch two holes in each side of the reinforced top of the bag and attach ribbon or twine handles.

A colorful sheet of newspaper or an old comic book makes an attractive bag.

TOP TIP
To make your bag more sturdy, cut out a piece of cardboard just smaller than the base and place it inside.

Old magazine

Knitting needle or skewer

Glue

Thread or elastic

Turn a magazine into a necklace

Creating paper beads is easy, and threading them together makes a stunning necklace or bracelet.

1 Cut out lots of long, thin triangles from the magazine pages. Make sure your triangles are all the same length and width.

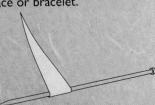

2 Starting at the widest end, tightly roll each triangle around a knitting needle. Dab a bit of glue on the narrow end to stick it down.

3 When the glue has dried and you have a collection of beads, thread them onto a piece of string or elastic to make your necklace.

Bowl

Plastic wrap or
petroleum jelly

Newspaper, cut into
strips (lots!)

White glue diluted
with the same
amount of water

Paints, colored
tissue paper, or
old wrapping paper
to decorate

Varnish

Make a decorative bowl

Papier mâché is a great way to transform old newspapers into decorative objects. A bowl is one of the easiest projects to start with—just remember, it won't be waterproof!

You can use your papier-mâché skills to make a piñata. See pages 70–71.

1 Wrap a bowl in plastic wrap or coat it with a layer of petroleum jelly. This will make it easier to release your creation once you're finished.

2 For the first layer, brush some newspaper strips with water and overlap them on the bowl, smoothing out any air bubbles.

3 Now use the diluted glue mixture to coat the paper and build up more layers, setting it aside to dry every few layers or so.

4 Remove from the mold and trim the edges to get a neat rim. Make a few final layers to neaten up the rim and the inside of your bowl.

5 When the bowl is completely dry, you can decorate it—see below for ideas. Add a layer of varnish when you're finished to protect your design.

TOP TIP
Make sure your strips aren't too wet or they won't dry flat. Wring out any excess liquid before sticking them on the bowl.

Use brightly colored candy wrappers, old magazines, or wrapping paper for a great decoupage effect.

Paint a white layer to hide the newspaper and make a base for your patterns.

Cut the paper into pieces, brush with undiluted glue, and stick down in patterns.

Try using colorful tissue paper instead of newspaper for your final layers of papier mâché.

Let your creativity run free and use paints to make fun designs.

Take a good photograph

With most modern cameras, you can just point and click. But you don't have to! Think a little before you press that button.

Automatic cameras usually focus on whatever is in the center of the frame. To get around this, aim at your subject, half press the button to focus, reframe creatively, and fully press the shutter.

Hold the camera steady with both hands or you'll get a blurry photo. Squeeze the button—don't jab it.

With people, make them laugh and relax, then take a lot of pictures and choose the best ones. If you have a zoom lens, zoom in a little to make faces look clearer.

Don't just put your subject in the middle. Off center can be more interesting.

Have fun with photography

Photography is an art form, capable of creating beautiful, moving, meaningful images. But, hey, lighten up. Forget all that art stuff. Mess around! Have fun! Try some of these ideas, and see if you can come up with a few of your own.

Fool with scale
If you get everything in focus, you can make a small foreground object look as big as a large background object. Line them up carefully, and you'll get a terrific effect.

Play with motion blur
To create dynamic images of a cyclist racing past, select a shady spot and turn off the flash. Follow the cyclist with the camera, pressing the button as he zooms by.

Mess around with a mirror
If you have a small mirror—ideally with no frame—you can use it to make crazy images of your friends with four eyes, two mouths, or even upside-down noses.

Snap a light picture

If you can set your camera to make a very long exposure, you can entertain yourself by drawing with light in the dark. You just need a darkened room and a flashlight, and somewhere to stand your camera. Check your camera instructions to find an option that gives a 15 to 20 second exposure.

1 Place the camera on a shelf, pointing into the middle of the room. Turn on your flashlight and turn off the lights. You want the room to be as dark as possible.

2 Press the button, stand back, and whirl your flashlight around while you count the seconds. Try to draw a pattern of light such as swirls or star shapes.

3 When you run out of moves, turn off the flashlight. Check the camera. If it is still recording, wait for it to stop. Then see what kind of image you've made. Wow!

LONG EXPOSURES

Normally a digital camera opens its shutter for a fraction of a second to make an exposure. To get longer exposures, you must either use manual mode—usually found only on big cameras—or a special "scene" mode designed for very dark conditions. Try things like "starry sky" or "fireworks"—or whatever mode your camera has that sounds similar.

TOP TIP
You can do these tricks with some film cameras, provided they have exposure controls. But printing costs may make this expensive.

TOP TIP
If your camera has a zoom lens, use the widest setting for tricks like these and everything will be in focus.

For more ghostly goings-on, turn to pages 28–29.

Scantastic!
Do you have a scanner attached to a computer? Try using it to photograph things like feathers, flowers, watches, and jewelry. But be careful not to scratch the glass plate.

Ghost effect
Get a friend to lurk in a spooky place for the first half of a 30-second exposure, then move quickly out of view. You'll need to support the camera and use the self-timer.

Pocket tripods like this are ideal for supporting small cameras.

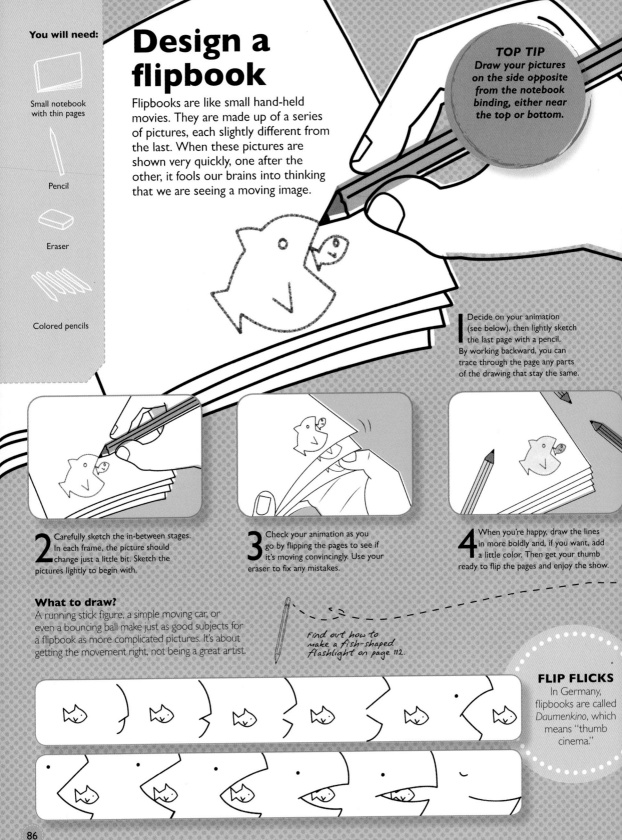

You will need:

Small notebook with thin pages

Pencil

Eraser

Colored pencils

Design a flipbook

Flipbooks are like small hand-held movies. They are made up of a series of pictures, each slightly different from the last. When these pictures are shown very quickly, one after the other, it fools our brains into thinking that we are seeing a moving image.

TOP TIP
Draw your pictures on the side opposite from the notebook binding, either near the top or bottom.

1 Decide on your animation (see below), then lightly sketch the last page with a pencil. By working backward, you can trace through the page any parts of the drawing that stay the same.

2 Carefully sketch the in-between stages. In each frame, the picture should change just a little bit. Sketch the pictures lightly to begin with.

3 Check your animation as you go by flipping the pages to see if it's moving convincingly. Use your eraser to fix any mistakes.

4 When you're happy, draw the lines in more boldly and, if you want, add a little color. Then get your thumb ready to flip the pages and enjoy the show.

What to draw?

A running stick figure, a simple moving car, or even a bouncing ball make just as good subjects for a flipbook as more complicated pictures. It's about getting the movement right, not being a great artist.

Find out how to make a fish-shaped flashlight on page 112.

FLIP FLICKS
In Germany, flipbooks are called *Daumenkino*, which means "thumb cinema."

You will need:

Computer with animation software

Digital camera

Tripod

Pencil

Modeling clay

Make a computer animation

Just like a flipbook, a computer animation is made up of many slightly different pictures. When these are played back quickly, it gives the illusion of movement. The animation software needed for this activity can be downloaded for free from the Internet.

1 Make your clay figure. For a snail, use a short, fat roll of clay for the body, a curled spiral for the shell, and two short stubby pieces for the antennae. Use the pencil to draw the snail's face.

2 Start up the animation software on your computer. Make sure your camera is attached to the computer via a cable and that the camera is on a tripod to keep it completely still.

3 Place your snail on a flat surface and frame it so that the snail's nose is just peeking into the left-hand side of the picture. Check the image on the computer screen and snap your picture.

4 Move the snail just a little bit so that more of it is in the shot. Your animation software should show a faint outline of the last picture, making it easier for you to line up.

5 Repeat. Keep moving the snail to the right until it disappears out of the shot. Check your progress to make sure everything is going smoothly and reshoot if you make a mistake.

6 Play back and enjoy your magical moving snail. Most animation programs also allow you to add sound and visual effects to your film.

More animation ideas

1 Frame by frame, create a spectacular toy car race around your living room with crashes, jumps, and lots of passes.

2 Take a picture of a friend standing still. Get them to move slightly forward and stand in the same position. Take another picture. Repeat. Your friend will magically glide across the floor.

3 Take a picture of a glass with a drink in it. Take a sip, and then place it back exactly where it was. Repeat. It will look as if the drink has been guzzled by an invisible monster.

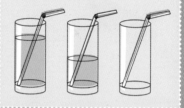

Thaumatrope

For a quick image trick, why not make a thaumatrope? This is a disk with an image on each side. The disk is attached to two pieces of string, which are twisted to make the disk spin around very quickly. When the disk spins fast enough, the eye can no longer tell the difference between the two images and sees a single image.

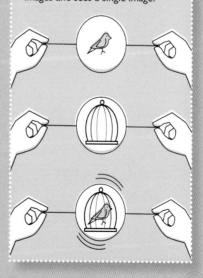

You will need:

16 x 16 in
(40 x 40 cm) sheet
of cardboard

White plastic
garbage bag

Fine-tipped pen

Colored markers
or acrylic paints

4 bamboo
skewers, each
10 in (25 cm) long

10 ft (3 m) plastic
or crepe streamers

50 ft (15 m) thin,
flexible nylon wire

String

Clear tape

4 in (10 cm) strong
cardboard tube

Make and fly a kite

People have been flying kites since long before the invention
of aircraft. There is a tradition of "fighting kites" in many
countries, with contestants glueing shards of glass to their
kite strings and attempting to cut the strings of their
opponents. We won't be doing that! But if you want,
you can build a lot of these inexpensive, easy-to-make
kites and fly them with your friends.

Flying your kite

1 Choose a breezy day.

2 Get a friend to hold the
kite the right way up. With
your back to the breeze,
walk back while unrolling
about 10 ft (3 m) of line.
When you are ready, ask
your friend to launch the
kite straight up into the air.

16 in (40 cm)

16 in (40 cm)

1 Make a cardboard template of a 16 x 16 in (40 x 40 cm) diamond sail. The vertical and horizontal lines shown above should meet 3 in (8 cm) from the top. This is the point where the two parts of your frame will meet.

2 Cut a sheet of plastic out of a garbage bag. Using your template, trace the outline onto the plastic and cut it out.

3 Fold your sail along the vertical and horizontal lines shown in step 1. Cut off the folded corner to make a small hole.

4 Decorate your kite with markers or acrylic paints. Use bold colors to make your kite stand out in the sky.

5 Tape two skewers together at the pointed ends to make the spine. It should be 0.2 in (5 mm) shorter than the sail.

6 Tape another two skewers together in the same way to make the crossbar. Lay the crossbar in place on the sail.

7 Tape the ends of the spine and crossbar to the sail, folding the plastic over the ends of the skewers.

8 Where the two sticks meet over the hole, tightly tie them together with string. Trim off any excess.

9 Take your nylon wire and tie one end to the cardboard tube. Roll the wire around the tube, then tie the loose end to the frame through the hole in the front of the kite.

10 Make a tail using lengths of plastic or crepe paper. Bunch them together and wrap the middle of them around the kite's spine, then tape in place. Up and away!

Streamers blow in the breeze and will look great when you're flying your kite.

Wrap the wire round a tube or stick to prevent it getting tangled.

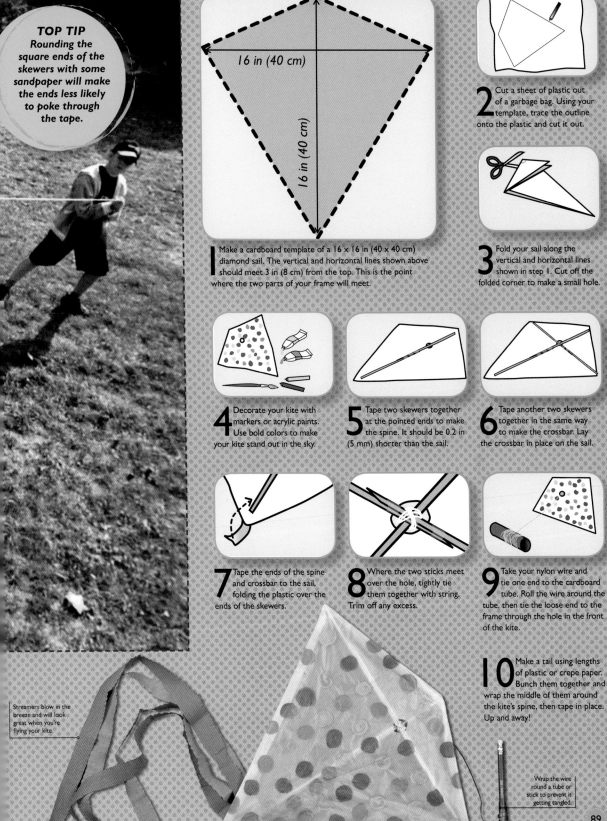

89

EXPLORE THE WORLD

Look closer at the natural world around you. Find out how to observe insects, attract birds, and plant seeds. Discover, too, the treasures of Earth and pan for gold, hunt for fossils, and learn how to grow your own crystals. And what about the rest of the universe? Gaze up into the sky and explore the mysterious Moon and the stars beyond.

Dig a pond

If you want wildlife in your backyard, the best way to attract it is to dig a pond. It doesn't need to be very big—just deep enough to avoid drying out or freezing solid if you have cold winters. Give it sloping sides so that animals can get in and out easily, and add pond plants to give animals somewhere to hide and improve the water quality.

You will need:

Digging tools

Sand and rocks

Old carpet and pond liner

Water and hose

Pond plants

1 Dig your hole in a sunny spot with no nearby trees. Make sure the middle is more than 32 in (80 cm) deep and that at least one side has a gentle slope. Make a shelf to support submerged plant pots.

2 Line the hole with sand, then cover this with pieces of old carpet. These will stop sharp stones from puncturing the pond liner. The color of the carpet doesn't matter, because it will be hidden.

3 Drape your pond liner over the hole with a big overlap all around. Put the end of the hose in the middle and turn it on. As the weight of the water increases, the liner will sink to fit the hole.

4 Carefully trim the edges of the liner. It's best if these turn up vertically for 6 in (15 cm) or so rather than lie flat. Hide them with a layer of rocks, add your pond plants, and wait for the wildlife to show up!

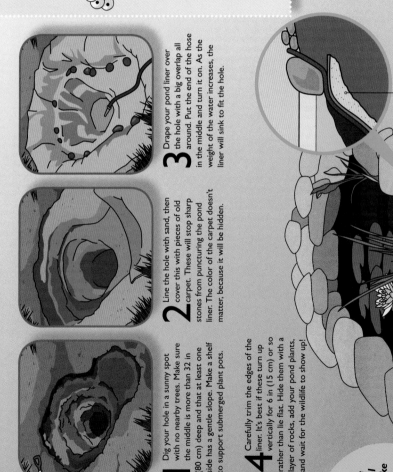

Arrange the sand (yellow), carpet (pink), and pond liner (dark gray) like this.

TOP TIP
Check your hole with a spirit level on a plank to make sure the sides are the same height or water will overflow on one side.

A frog's life cycle

You may be lucky enough to discover that frogs have moved into your pond—so it's worth knowing the life cycle of these fascinating creatures.

5 The frogs hunt small animals near the pond. When full grown, they will breed in the pond.

4 After their front legs appear, the tails shrink and they become miniature frogs.

3 In time they grow small back legs, but they still have long tails and live underwater.

1 Adult frogs lay round jelly-covered eggs called frog spawn.

2 The eggs become tiny tadpoles with feathery gills. They grow fatter and fatter as they feed among the pondweed.

POND ECOSYSTEM

A pond is a miniature ecosystem. Pond animals breathe oxygen released by pond plants, which make their stems and leaves using carbon dioxide produced by animals. In the mud, microbes turn animal waste into nutrients for the plants. The entire ecosystem gets its energy from the Sun.

Identify carnivorous plants

Many animals eat plants, but some plants survive by eating visiting insects! These plants live in places such as acid peat bogs where the soil contains very few nutrients of the type found in fertile soil. So they get the nutrients they need by catching and digesting small animals. Don't keep these plants in a tank with a lid on or their prey won't be able to get in.

Pitcher plant
This has modified leaves that contain liquid. Insects tumble into the liquid and drown. Their bodies are digested and absorbed by the plant.

Sundew
Sticky hairs on a sundew trap insects as they land. The plant slowly bends its hairs over the insects, and digestive juices dissolve their bodies.

Venus flytrap
Each leaf is a hinged trap, sprung by tiny hairlike triggers on the leaf's surface. The trap snaps shut in a split second, and there is no escape.

Butterwort
Despite its pretty flowers, this bog plant is a killer. It has sticky leaves that snare insects and release fluids that turn their victims into plant food.

Set up a terrarium

You can set up your very own self-sufficient ecosystem in your home, in an enclosed glass container called a terrarium. The idea is to raise a variety of plants that all like the same conditions, such as the warmth and moisture of a tropical swamp. There will be microscopic animals living alongside the plants, but you won't be able to see them!

It's best if the lid is transparent, so that the plants get plenty of light.

Once you get the moisture level right, the plants shouldn't to be watered.

Everything the plants need is inside the terrarium, so it's self-sufficient.

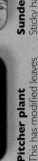

You will need:

Glass tank with tight-fitting lid

Activated carbon (from pet stores)

Clean gravel and potting compost

Miniature plants

Grow plants from seeds on pages 100–101

1 Put a 1 in (25 mm) layer of gravel in the bottom of the tank. Add a 0.25 in (6 mm) layer of activated carbon, then a 2 in (50 mm) layer of a potting compost suitable for your plants.

2 Find a good arrangement for your plants, then plant them in the compost. Water them lightly and put the lid on. Put your terrarium in a place that gets plenty of indirect sunlight.

3 Congratulations, you've created an ecosystem! Keep checking it to gauge whether or not the moisture levels are correct. If the compost starts to dry out, add a little water. If there seems to be too much water, forming thick condensation on the glass, remove the lid for half an hour. Then put it back on.

3 pieces of wood,
0.6 x 0.6 in
(15 x 15 mm),
cut into 2 x
8.3 in (210 mm)
and 1 x 10.5 in
(267 mm) lengths

4 bulldog clips

2 sheets of perspex

Plastic wrap

Thick paper

Ants

Keep ants

Ants are amazing creatures that live in complex colonies centered around a breeding queen. The worker ants look after the queen's eggs and young, gather food, and fight off enemies. Make your own ant farm and see them in action.

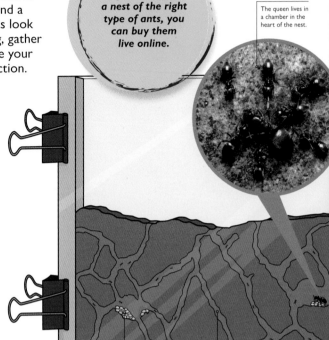

TOP TIP
If you can't find a nest of the right type of ants, you can buy them live online.

The queen lives in a chamber in the heart of the nest.

1 Glue the two shorter pieces of wood to the ends of the longer one, forming a U shape (see picture). When dry, clip the perspex sheets to each side.

2 Ask an adult who knows about insects to help you find a nest of black ants and carefully collect some. You need worker ants, white larvae, the queen, and some eggs.

3 Pour soil into your ant farm until it is two thirds full, then add the ants. Give them some chopped ripe fruit or honey-soaked bread to eat. Soak some cotton wool in water and drop that in, too.

4 Seal the top of the box with plastic wrap pierced with pinholes. Tape thick paper around the farm so that the ants can build their nest in the dark, but take it off from time to time to look into their fascinating world.

White larvae

The ants build long tunnels, with chambers for eggs and larvae.

Transparent tank (with a thin, plastic lid, if possible)

Pin or nail for making holes in the lid

Paper and thick card

Butterfly eggs or caterpillars

Raise caterpillars

Many insects, such as butterflies, start life as wingless soft-bodied larvae that eat all the time, grow fast, and finally turn into beautiful winged adults. You can watch this process by raising some caterpillars.

TOP TIP
Butterflies are picky about where they lay eggs, so check an insect book to see where you should be looking for their eggs and caterpillars.

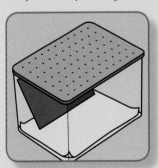

1 Make 30–40 small holes in the lid to let plenty of air in. If you don't have a lid, mesh or plastic wrap (with holes) will work. Put paper on the floor of the tank and lean a piece of cardboard against the back for the pupae to cling onto later.

2 Next hunt for caterpillars, or their eggs, often laid in small groups on leaves. Gather the leaves you find them on, too, and put them in a jar of water. Place the leaves and the eggs or caterpillars in the tank.

3 As the caterpillars eat the leaves, add more. Keep the water jar full and regularly change the paper to remove any caterpillar droppings. Eventually, the caterpillars will climb onto the cardboard or lid and turn into non-feeding pupae.

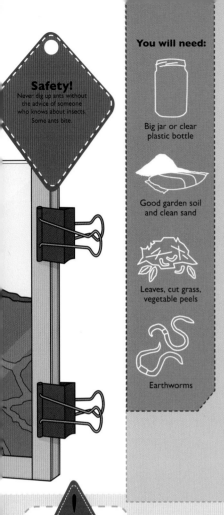

You will need:

Big jar or clear plastic bottle

Good garden soil and clean sand

Leaves, cut grass, vegetable peels

Earthworms

Farm worms

Earthworms may not seem like very exciting animals, but we need them. They churn up and aerate the soil, create vital plant food, and turn barren dirt into rich, fertile soil. Keep some in a jar to watch them at work.

1 Add a layer of soil roughly 2 in (5 cm) deep. Firm it down and add a thin layer of sand. Repeat, building up the layers, until you are 2 in (5 cm) from the top. Make sure the top layer is soil. If you don't have a big jar, cut the top off a large, clear plastic bottle and use that instead.

2 Cover the surface with leaves, grass, and vegetable peels for food and place the worms on top. Keep your farm somewhere dark, but regularly examine it and you'll see the layers disappear as the worms work the soil.

The worms mix the soil as they swallow and excrete it.

The vegetation is dragged down into the soil, where it breaks down faster.

American monarch butterflies lay eggs on milkweed leaves.

4 After about ten days, the case of each pupa will split open to reveal the miraculous transformation as a butterfly wiggles out. It won't look like much at first, because its wings will be crumpled up.

5 Watch carefully and you will see each butterfly slowly "pump up" its wings to their full glory. After a few hours, the wings will have dried out, and it will be able to fly. Let it go so that it can fly off to find a mate and produce more eggs and caterpillars.

Butterfly life cycle

An adult female butterfly lays an egg that hatches as a tiny leaf-eating caterpillar. This grows bigger and bigger until it forms a pupa—the transition stage where it turns into an adult butterfly.

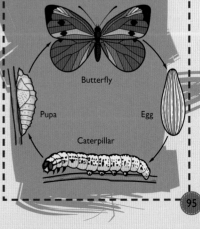

Butterfly

Pupa

Egg

Caterpillar

Catch fireflies

Fireflies are flying beetles that live in warm regions. They emit light, flashing messages at one another on summer evenings. If fireflies are common where you live, you can catch some and use them to make a living lantern.

You will need:

Clean glass jar with a metal screw-top lid

Paper towels

Sharp nail and hammer

Block of scrap wood, several short sticks, and 2–3 leaves

Butterfly net

Fireflies

1 Use the hammer and nail to make five or six holes in the lid of your jar. Turn it over and hammer the sharp edges flat.

2 Wet the paper towels, squeeze out the water, and lay them on the bottom of the jar with the sticks and leaves on top.

3 Use your net to catch some fireflies. Put them in the jar and screw on the lid. If you collect enough, you will light your way through the dark. Set the fireflies free at the end of the evening.

Fireflies glow with cold light created by a chemical reaction.

To make the fireflies feel at home in the jar, add some sticks and leaves. Make sure these do not reach more than halfway up the jar.

Attract and feed moths

When the sun goes down, a lot of wildlife wakes up. This is especially true of most moths, which fly only at night. Some are beautiful, but we rarely see them. You can get a closer look using techniques to attract moths, such as offering a tempting meal of fermenting fruit.

You will need:

Overripe fruit (ask your local grocery store)

1 cup brown sugar

1 teaspoon dry yeast

Old sponge

Flashlight and digital camera with flash

1 Mash the fruit in a bowl, then mix in the sugar and add just enough water to dissolve the sugar. Add the yeast and cover the mixture.

2 Put the mixture in a warm place for a few days. The fruit will ferment, releasing a scent that moths find irresistible.

3 Use the sponge to spread some of the aromatic mixture on a few nearby tree trunks that you can easily visit at night.

4 When it gets dark, visit each tree and check the bait using a flashlight. Use your camera to record any moths you attract.

TOP TIP
Another way of attracting moths is to use a flashlight to illuminate a white sheet. Moths will be drawn toward the light.

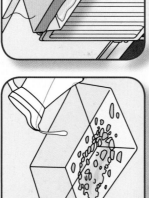

Dissect an owl pellet

Owls are night hunters that normally swallow small prey whole. They cough up bones, feathers, and fur in the form of compact pellets that collect beneath owl roosts. If you find a pellet, you can dissect it to see what the owl has eaten.

Look out for owls

Owls hunt in the dark using their super-sensitive hearing and their big eyes, which can see in the dimmest light. Listen for their hooting calls while you are out at night looking for moths and fireflies, and shine your flashlight up into tree branches. You might pick out an unexpected visitor flying overhead!

Shoulder blades

Front leg bones

Hipbones

Back leg bones

Vertebrae

Ribs

You will need:

Disposable gloves and disinfectant

Small plastic container and shallow dish

Absorbent paper

Tweezers and toothpicks

Magnifying glass

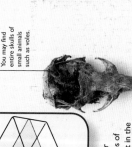

1 Half fill the plastic container with water. Add a few drops of disinfectant. Place the pellet in the container and soak it until it sinks.

You may find entire skulls of small animals such as voles.

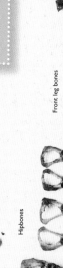

2 Take the pellet out, dry it a little, place it in the tray, and carefully break it apart with your tweezers and toothpicks.

3 Remove any bones or similar items, put them on the paper to dry, and try to identify them with your magnifying glass.

Learn how to hoot like an owl on page 151

Birdseed, dried fruit, bread crumbs

Lard

Saucepan and spoon

Plastic yogurt pot

2 ft (60 cm) string

Cook for birds

You can enjoy wonderful views of birds by offering them food. Birdseed will attract seed-eating birds, but birds that eat small animals need different foods. Try making a cake of seeds mixed with lard—a form of animal fat that gives birds the nutrients they need.

1 Mix together the birdseed, bread crumbs, and dried fruit. Melt the lard in a heated saucepan and add the seed mixture. Stir it well and let it cool a little.

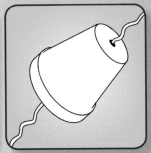

2 Poke a small hole in the bottom of the yogurt container. Tie a knot 6 in (15 cm) from the end of the string and pull the other end through the hole until you get to the knot.

3 Spoon the contents of the saucepan into the yogurt container, filling it to the top. Put it on a plate in case it leaks a little and leave it in a cool place overnight to harden.

Use seeds that are meant for wild birds to make your cake.

Adding a perch will help smaller birds to get a grip.

4 Carefully remove the yogurt container. The mixture should have hardened around the string. Use this to hang the cake from a tree or bird-feeding station.

Watch more wildlife on pages 150–151.

Fill a pine cone

Here's an even easier way to make a birdfeeder that doesn't involve cooking. Filling a pinecone with food that birds love not only encourages them to feed acrobatically, it also gives anyone watching them a treat.

1 Tie a length of string around the base of the pinecone.

2 Smear peanut butter over the cone, pushing it far into the cracks. Then roll it in birdseed so that the seeds stick to the peanut butter. Hang the food-packed cone from a branch.

TOP TIP
Regularly clean out feeders and move them around to stop disease-carrying bird droppings from building up beneath them.

You will need:

Large, clear plastic bottle with screw cap

Drill

Large plastic jar cap

Paper napkin

Glue gun

Screw hook

Sugar and water

Red plastic flowers and ribbons

Make a hummingbird feeder

If you are lucky enough to live in a region where hummingbirds fly regularly through your garden, try making a feeder to attract them near a window where you can watch them.

Important!
You will need adult help using the drill and glue gun. Also, be sure to rinse out the feeder every three days and thoroughly clean it once a week.

1 Drill a ring of holes in the bottle cap, then punch through the plastic connecting the holes to create one large hole. The more holes you drill, the easier this is!

2 Stuff the napkin in the hole so that it sticks out a little. Place the bottle cap upside down in the center of the larger jar cap, resting on the napkin. Make sure it is level.

3 Use the glue gun to create four wide "bridges" joining the outer and inner caps. You will need to apply several layers of glue. Be sure to leave spaces between the bridges.

4 Allow the glue to harden, then remove the napkin. Drill a small hole in the base of the bottle and insert the screw hook. Seal around it with more glue. You will use this to hang the feeder.

5 To make the "nectar," mix one part sugar with four parts water and heat it until the sugar dissolves. Let this cool, then pour it into the bottle until half full. Gently screw on the cap.

6 Turn the bottle upside down. The nectar should make a small pool in the cap, while most of it stays in the bottle. Decorate the feeder with red ribbon and plastic flowers and hang it up.

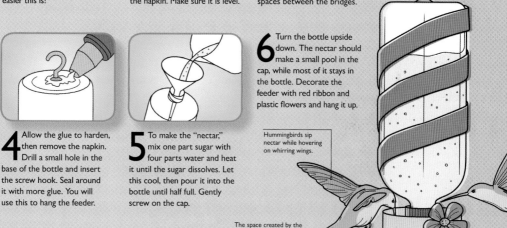

Hummingbirds sip nectar while hovering on whirring wings.

The space created by the napkin between the two caps allows the nectar to fill the jar cap while the birds feed.

Hang a bird box

A great way to encourage small birds to your area is to put up a nest box. Choose one to suit the birds you like and follow these tips.

Do

• Hang the bird box at least 6.5 ft (2 m) above the ground, out of reach of cats.

• Put up two or three boxes close together if you want, but only if they are for birds that like company. If not, put up just one box for a single pair.

• Clean out the box at the end of the nesting season and pour boiling water over the inside to kill any bugs.

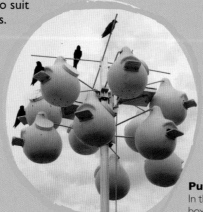

Don't

• Don't put it up just anywhere. The birds won't use it if it gets too hot, so make sure it is in the shade by midday and throughout the afternoon, when the sun is at its warmest.

• Don't put it near a bird-feeding area, because nesting birds don't like being disturbed by other birds.

• Don't use insecticides or other chemicals to clean the box.

Purple martin nest boxes
In the U.S., many people put up multiple boxes for nesting purple martins.

Watch a bean sprout

Though we don't tend to think of them as intelligent, plants are extremely smart when it comes to surviving. In the right conditions, they are able to find their own sources of water and stretch toward the sky to find sunlight, which they then use to make their own food. See it happen for yourself.

BEST BEANS
The easiest beans and seeds for sprouting are alfalfa, flax, lentil, mung, soy, and sunflower.

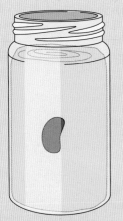

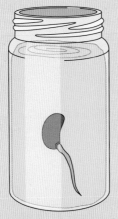

4 Watch the shoot grow taller. You will see more roots and then leaves appear. Your sprout has become a bean plant.

The bean grows leaves to absorb more light for food.

The stem transports water from the root and keeps the plant upright.

More and more roots appear as the plant grows.

1 Roll up some paper towels and pack them into a jar. Pour in some water, to the height of about 1 in (2.5 cm), and place a dried bean halfway up the jar.

2 Keep the jar in a bright, warm place. After a few days, watch as a root appears and grows downward to reach the water source. Top up the jar with water regularly.

3 After a few more days, you will see a shoot sprout upward, away from the root. It is looking for sunlight, which it needs to make food in a process called photosynthesis.

Build a compost pile

Mother Nature is the greatest recycler of us all, but if you give her a hand, you can benefit from her hard work. By keeping your waste material together, microorganisms such as fungi, yeasts, and bacteria will break it down into compost, which you can use to fertilize your garden.

1 You can use any container to hold your compost—it just needs to keep the compost warm and prevent rats and mice from getting in. The best place to put it is on bare soil in a sunny place.

2 As you add items to your compost, try to get a 50/50 mix of "green" and "brown" layers to provide the perfect environment for microorganisms. Don't include cooked food, fish, dairy products, or meat since these will attract rats and mice.

3 A year after you start, check if the compost is brown and crumbly at the bottom (the oldest compost). If it is, you can use it in your garden.

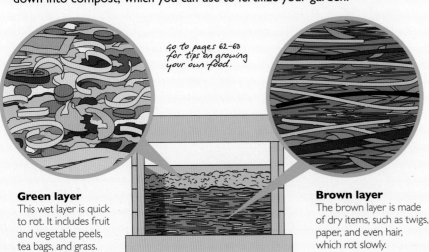

Go to pages 62–63 for tips on growing your own food.

Green layer
This wet layer is quick to rot. It includes fruit and vegetable peels, tea bags, and grass.

Brown layer
The brown layer is made of dry items, such as twigs, paper, and even hair, which rot slowly.

TOP TIP
The more varied the ingredients, the better your compost will be.

Grow apples

Those little brown seeds around the core of an apple are not just there to get stuck in your teeth—they are seeds that you can use to grow an apple tree, although it will take several years.

1 Dry some apple seeds, place them on a damp paper towel, fold it into quarters, and put it in a plastic bag in the fridge. After about six weeks, some seeds should start to sprout.

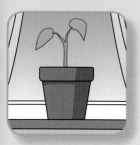

2 Bury the seeds in plant pots filled with soil. Place the pots somewhere bright and keep the soil moist. Repot the plants as they grow and move them outside.

3 If you've done everything right, you could be gathering your own apples after a few years. The tree may even outlive you!

You will need:

Sunflower seeds

Garden fork

Garden compost or fertilizer

Water

Sturdy canes

String

Plant some sunflower seeds

Vibrant and beautiful, sunflowers come in all shapes and sizes and can even be grown inside. Before you start, it's a good idea to think about how much room you have and then go for the variety that best suits you—some sunflowers can stretch to more than 10 ft (3 m) tall, but the smaller ones can be under 3 ft (1 m).

1 Find a suitable container in a sunny spot—the bigger the pot, the better the chance your flower will be a giant. Work some compost or fertilizer into the soil and plant the seeds. Cover with soil and press down firmly.

2 Sunflowers love water, so make sure the soil is always moist. Watch the plant as it grows—the stem and leaves will appear after a few weeks, with the flower forming a few more weeks after that.

3 As the plant grows, you may need to secure it with a cane and some string to keep it upright. The flower heads can get quite heavy, and the wind can blow over an unsecured plant.

4 When the flowering period is over, cut the flower with about 4 in (10 cm) stalk attached and hang it up to dry in a well-ventilated area. When it is completely dry, the seeds will pop out easily. You can eat these as a healthy snack or feed them to the birds, but save some seeds to plant next year.

You will need:

Thick, strong polyester rope and an equal length of light throwing line to reach up to the branch and back

Non-breakable soft weight such as an old sock filled with sand

Bicycle helmet or similar

Clean tire

Drill

Important!
You will need an adult to operate the drill, help you choose a good branch, and test the swing before you use it.

TOP TIP
If you ever need to remove the rope from the tree, untie the tire and pull down on the throwing line.

Make a tire swing

If you have a big tree with spreading branches in your yard, you are probably itching to make a tire swing. How do you get the rope up the tree without risking your life climbing up there? Here's how!

1 Tie the rope to one end of the throwing line using a double sheet bend knot (see page 148). Tie the other end of the line to the weight. Wearing the helmet, toss the weight over a branch.

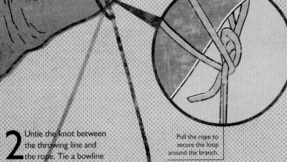

Pull the rope to secure the loop around the branch.

2 Untie the knot between the throwing line and the rope. Tie a bowline knot (see page 149) at the end of the rope to create a loop and tie the throwing line to it. Pass the other end of the rope through the loop and tug on it to pull the loop up and around the branch.

3 Drill three holes close together in the tread of the tire and turn so that the holes are at the bottom for drainage. Tie the tire to your hanging rope using a round turn knot (see page 148). Cut off any spare rope or store it inside the tire.

4 Tie the hanging throwing line around the tree and out of the way. You are now ready to start swinging!

4 To come down, relax the grip of your feet and slide them down the rope as you let yourself down hand over hand. Use your feet as a brake. Never just slide down or the friction will burn the skin on your hands.

Climb slowly and steadily—if you rush you may slip.

3 Release the grip of your feet slightly and bring your knees up to your chest while allowing the rope to slip between your feet. Then grip the rope again with your feet. "Stand up" on the rope and reach up again with your arms. Keep going like this.

2 Wrap the rope around one leg and hold it between your feet. Relax your arms slightly to see if your feet are supporting you. If they are, reach up to just above your head and grasp the rope securely.

Climb only low heights until you gain confidence.

1 Jump up and grab the rope with your hands. Pull yourself up as far as you can.

Climb a rope

Have you ever tried to climb a rope but just kept slipping down? This is the technique to get you to the top.

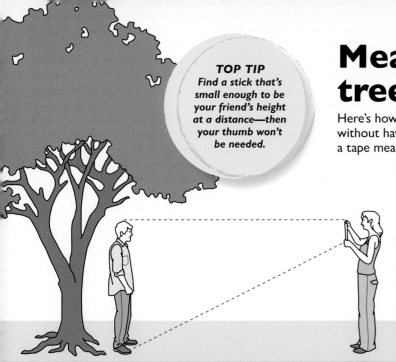

TOP TIP
Find a stick that's small enough to be your friend's height at a distance—then your thumb won't be needed.

Measure a tree's height

Here's how to measure how tall a tree is without having to climb it. You just need a tape measure, a friend, a stick, and math.

1 Measure your friend's height with a tape measure. Walk away until you can see the entire tree. Hold a stick upright at arm's length so that its top end is level with the top of your friend's head, then move your hand so that your thumb is level with his or her feet.

2 Staying in the same position, measure how many times the stick's length, from your thumb to its top, can be placed end to end until you reach the treetop.

3 Now for the math. Multiply your friend's height by the amount of times the stick goes into the tree's height. If your friend was 5 ft (1.5 m) tall and the stick went end to end eight times, the tree's height is 8 x 5 ft (1.5 m) = 40 ft (12 m).

Figure out a tree's age

Some trees have very long lives. The oldest-known living tree—a bristlecone pine growing in California—is an astonishing 5,000 years old. That's older than Stonehenge! Discover the age of trees near you by hugging them with a tape measure.

1 Since a tree adds a thin layer of wood to its trunk every year, the trunk gets thicker and thicker. Choose a tree with a trunk that is much broader (and thus older) than those of similar trees nearby.

2 To get some idea of just how old it is, take a tape measure and find the girth (distance around the trunk) in inches or centimetres approximately 39 in (1 m) from the ground.

3 Then divide the girth by 1 in (2.5 cm)—the average amount that the trunk grows per year. So, if the girth is 300 in (750 cm), dividing this by 1 in (2.5 cm) gives 300 years. However, this is only a minimum age, and the tree could easily be twice as old!

TREE-RING DATING

Tree rings vary in width depending on whether the tree had a good summer or not. A ring from a good year is thicker than a ring from a bad year. Each year is different, and each decade or even century has a sequence unique to a time and place. Dendrochronologists are scientists who can match these sequences with patterns in timber using computers. They then know when the tree grew and where.

Trees in areas with cold winters and hot summers have visible growth rings. Tropical trees do not have these rings because they grow all the time.

The tree adds dark-colored wood later in the growing season.

Light-colored wood is added earlier in the growing season.

If you count the number of rings from the middle to the edge, you come up with the age of the tree.

Broad, shallow metal or plastic pan

Shallow, rocky upland stream

Pan for gold

Gold prospectors still use this ancient technique to find deposits of gold in streams. Swirling water through the streambed material washes away the lighter mud and stones, leaving the heaviest grains, which may include the heaviest of all—gold!

Safety!
Be careful not to trespass on someone's property, especially if the area is known for its gold deposits. You might violate someone's mining rights and be arrested.

How to pan for gold

1 In the stream, find a bed of sand and fine gravel. Scoop some of it into your pan until it is about three-quarters full.

2 Sit on a rock with your feet in about 6 in (15 cm) of running water. Submerge your pan and stir the contents with your fingers to wash out any mud.

3 Shake the pan side to side underwater. Sweep out any lighter stones with your hand until only fine material is left.

4 Tilt the pan and swirl beneath the surface to let the water carry away lighter grains. Shake the pan so that the heavier grains sink.

5 Eventually, you will have only the heaviest minerals. Look out for shiny yellow flecks of gold.

You will need:

Triangular wire coat hanger

Wire cutters

Dowse for water

For centuries, some people have claimed an ability to dowse, or divine, for water—using rods or pendulums to find water. There is no scientific explanation for why dowsing may work or why it works for some people and not others. See if it works for you.

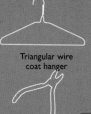

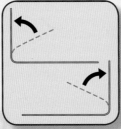

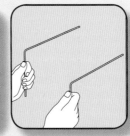

1 Cut through the middle of each side of the hanger. Discard the hooked part and keep the two bent sides.

2 Pull open one bent side until you have an L-shaped rod. Do the same to the other bent side.

3 Hold the rods loosely in your hands, with the longer part facing forward and slightly down.

4 Walk towards a bucket of water. The free ends of the rods should cross over above the water.

Hunt for fossils

Fossils are the remains of ancient living things that have been preserved instead of decaying. They are usually stony, and you can often find them near coastal cliffs and other places where soft rocks have been worn away.

Safety!
Stay away from unstable cliffs and beware of the tide if you are searching on a beach.

2 Try splitting large, layered soft rocks with a geological hammer to see any fossils inside. Use eye protection.

1 Find a known fossil site. Don't look in the cliff itself, but search the debris that has fallen from it. Check rocks for fossils on their surfaces and search gravel beds for fossils that have broken free.

3 If you find a fossil in a rock fragment, don't try to chip it out. If the rock is too heavy to carry, take a photo instead.

Common fossils

Ammonites were marine mollusks with spiral shells.

Squidlike belemnites died out at the same time as the dinosaurs.

You can often find perfectly preserved shark's teeth.

This ancient bivalve fossil is similar to a modern oyster.

You will need:

Goggles

Strong leather gloves

Flint

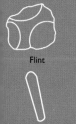
Heavy hammerstone

Metal flaking tool

1 Chip away at the flint with the hammerstone to remove the white outer layer, then try to knock off a big triangular flake.

2 Place this on a hard surface and use the hammerstone to roughly shape it by knocking smaller flakes off the edges.

Knap flint

Try a skill that has been known for at least one million years to make a sharp-edged stone tool. The ideal stone for this is flint—a hard stone that is a lot like black glass.

Flint axes were used for cutting timber and smaller blades for cutting and scraping.

3 At this stage, grind off any sharp edges with a piece of hard, rough stone. This makes shaping the flint easier.

4 Sharpen the edges by using your metal tool to remove small flakes. Apply pressure with a rolling, downward motion.

5 Use a smaller tool to neaten the edges and make them really sharp, but be careful not to cut yourself on your creation.

Safety!
Keep your hands clear of the area where the hammerstone will fall. Wear eye protection at all times to stop chips of stone from flying into your eyes.

Liquid detergent
and glycerin

Big bowl and bucket

Wire coat
hangers and pliers

Blow beautiful bubbles

Though they are fun to make and very pretty to look at, normal soap bubbles tend to be quite small and pop very easily. However, if you apply a little bit of science to the situation, you can create giant bubbles that last a lot longer. All it takes is the right recipe of detergent, water, and glycerin. The detergent and water make the bubbles big, and the glycerin stops the water from evaporating (which makes bubbles burst). These bubbles are so big and tough that you can even blow more bubbles inside them!

The changing colors and patterns on the surface are caused by light reflecting and refracting off the inside and outside of the bubble.

TOP TIP
The round shapes of six-pack drink holders, toilet paper tubes, and even your own hands can be used for blowing bubbles.

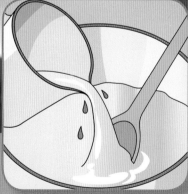

1 To make your extra-strength bubble mixture, add two parts of glycerin to 15 parts of liquid detergent. Then slowly add 15 parts of water and stir gently to mix. You don't want to create foam.

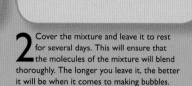

2 Cover the mixture and leave it to rest for several days. This will ensure that the molecules of the mixture will blend thoroughly. The longer you leave it, the better it will be when it comes to making bubbles.

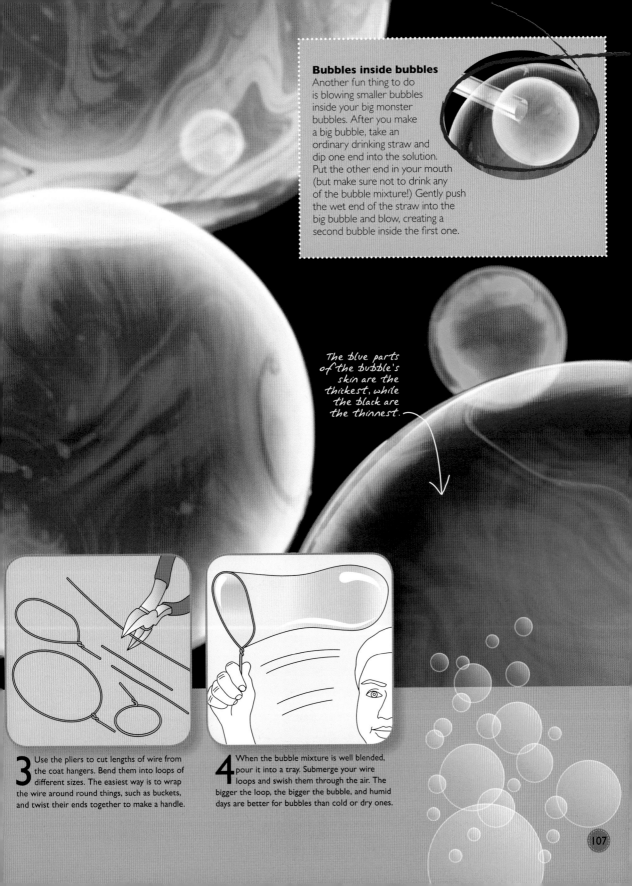

Bubbles inside bubbles
Another fun thing to do is blowing smaller bubbles inside your big monster bubbles. After you make a big bubble, take an ordinary drinking straw and dip one end into the solution. Put the other end in your mouth (but make sure not to drink any of the bubble mixture!) Gently push the wet end of the straw into the big bubble and blow, creating a second bubble inside the first one.

The blue parts of the bubble's skin are the thickest, while the black are the thinnest.

3 Use the pliers to cut lengths of wire from the coat hangers. Bend them into loops of different sizes. The easiest way is to wrap the wire around round things, such as buckets, and twist their ends together to make a handle.

4 When the bubble mixture is well blended, pour it into a tray. Submerge your wire loops and swish them through the air. The bigger the loop, the bigger the bubble, and humid days are better for bubbles than cold or dry ones.

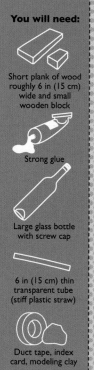

Short plank of wood roughly 6 in (15 cm) wide and small wooden block

Strong glue

Large glass bottle with screw cap

6 in (15 cm) thin transparent tube (stiff plastic straw)

Duct tape, index card, modeling clay

Mineral oil (such as baby oil)

Build a barometer

Changes in the weather are related to changes in pressure in the atmosphere. As warm air rises, it creates low-pressure zones with clouds and rain. By contrast, cool air sinks, resulting in high pressure, which stops clouds from forming, making the weather fine. You can measure these changes with a simple barometer.

1 Glue the block to one end of the plank. Tape the bottle to the plank with the mouth about 4 in (10 cm) from the block.

2 Insert the tube into the bottle, leaving it just above the block, and seal it to the mouth with modeling clay.

3 Slip the bottle cap under the end of the tube so that it forms a small cup, with the tube ending just above the bottom.

4 Glue a blank index card behind the tube. Fill the cup with mineral oil— some of the oil will creep up the tube.

5 Carefully carry your barometer to a cool, shady place and support it upright. Mark the oil levels on the card from day to day. Higher air pressure raises the level of oil in the tube—good weather. If pressure is low, rain may be on the way.

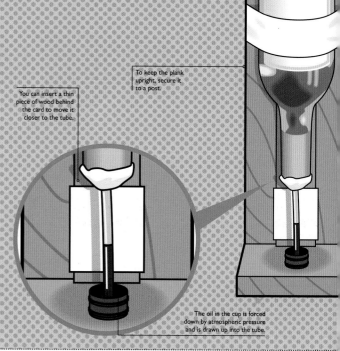

You can insert a thin piece of wood behind the card to move it closer to the tube.

To keep the plank upright, secure it to a post.

The oil in the cup is forced down by atmospheric pressure and is drawn up into the tube.

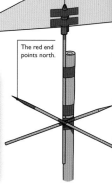

Waterproof piece of cardboard

2 coins

Tape

Red pen and pointed pen cap

3 wooden skewers

Long garden cane

Wire

Make a weathervane

When a low-pressure weather system is bringing bad weather your way, it makes the wind change. You can watch for these wind shifts using a weathervane, which points toward the direction from which the wind is blowing.

The skewer fits inside the pen cap at the balance point, allowing it to turn freely in any direction.

The red end points north.

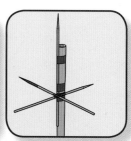

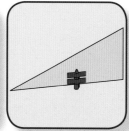

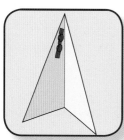

1 Fold the cardboard lengthwise and cut it to make a long folded triangle. Then tape two small coins side by side inside the triangle near the tip.

2 Tape the triangle together. Hold lightly between your index finger and thumb until the triangle doesn't tip. Make a mark at that point and tape the pen cap at the mark.

3 Tape one skewer to the cane, with the pointed end at the top. Wire the other two skewers in a cross shape just below the top of the cane.

4 Color one arm of the cross red. Add the vane and check that it spins. Push the cane into the ground and turn it so that red points north.

Measure rainfall

Rainfall is measured using a rain gauge, which is a parallel-sided container marked with a scale. It is easy to make your own from a plastic bottle, using a ruler as the scale. To get accurate readings, you have to fill the bottom of the bottle, mark the level, and then measure any water added by rainfall every day.

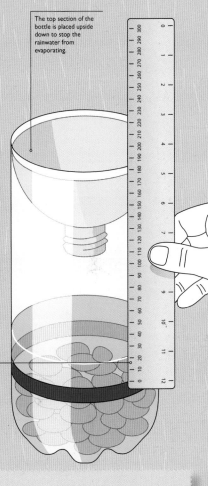

The top section of the bottle is placed upside down to stop the rainwater from evaporating.

1 Cut the top off the bottle at the point where its curved shoulders join the straight sides. Try to make a neat cut. Save both parts of the bottle.

2 Mark the base of the parallel part of the bottle with tape and fill the bottom with pebbles. Turn the top of the bottle upside down and insert it like a funnel.

3 Fill with water to the top of the tape marker. This is the zero point. Put the rain gauge outside, and after it rains, use the ruler to measure the height of water above the tape. Then pour water out until the level matches the top of the tape again.

Record the measurement in a notebook to build up a picture of rainfall in your area.

TOP TIP
Check the rain gauge every day to make sure that the water level does evaporate. If it does, fill it up to zero again.

Identify clouds

Clouds are created when invisible water vapor in rising air cools and condenses to form tiny airborne droplets of liquid water. It does this at different heights to form many different types of clouds, some of which bring rain. Here are four of the most important:

Cirrus
Thin, wispy cirrus clouds are made of tiny ice crystals, often in long trails. They always form high up in the sky, where the air is very cold.

Stratus
Flat sheets of low-level stratus clouds form in low-pressure weather systems. They make the sky gray, but do not usually bring rain.

Cumulus
These fluffy white clouds often form in good weather as warm, moist air rises into the cool blue sky. They can grow into storm clouds.

Cumulonimbus
If there is enough moisture in the air, this can form huge clouds that grow to more than 6 miles (10 km) high and cause thunderstorms.

Grow mineral crystals

Minerals are the chemical compounds that make up rocks. Many minerals can dissolve in water, and if the water dries out, the minerals are left behind as beautiful natural crystals that look like glittering gems. You can grow your own crystals using hot water and a mineral called alum, which you can buy at hardware and grocery stores.

1 Pour some hot water into a jar and stir in about three spoonfuls of alum powder, one at a time. Use one spoon to measure the alum and another to stir. Add more alum until it stops dissolving. Cover the jar and leave overnight.

2 As it cools, the water cannot hold as much alum in solution. Some of it turns solid again and forms small crystals at the bottom of the jar. Pour the alum solution into the second jar, but save the crystals that have formed.

3 Pick out the biggest and best crystal. Loop the end of the fishing line around the crystal and tie a knot to hold it in place. Tie the other end around a pencil and suspend it in the middle of a new jar of alum solution.

4 Cover again and leave for several days. If you've done it right, more alum will cling to your suspended crystal, making it grow bigger and bigger. You should end up with a real beauty!

Make gooey slime

There are some substances that defy the usual laws about what is solid and what is liquid—they're called antithixotropic. They act like liquids in normal conditions, but when you squeeze them, they become firmer and more solid, only to become gooey and slimy again when you release them.

1 Fill a cup with cornstarch and tip it into the bowl. Slowly add about half a cup of water, stirring all the time. You should end up with a gooey mixture.

2 Add a few drops of food coloring and stir until the mixture is all the same color. You could add some glitter, too, if you want.

3 Add some more cornstarch to thicken the mixture until you can roll it like dough between your hands. Shape it into a ball. You're done!

You will need:

Diet cola

Package of mints

Explode cola with mints

For complex reasons, some types of mint candies have a dramatic effect on carbonated drinks, especially diet cola, triggering the explosive release of all of the carbon dioxide that gives the drink its fizz. You can try it yourself, but be prepared to run fast!

All shapes and colors

If you suspend a shape made from pipe cleaners in the alum solution, the crystals should attach themselves to it. You can could add food coloring to the mix or paint the crystals afterward for even more design fun! If you make a few, you can create a simple mobile by joining them together.

COOL SCIENCE
The science behind substances like this one has been used to make things such as protective sportswear, body armor, and soccer balls.

1 Carefully open the cola bottle and place it down on concrete. Take four mints from the package.

2 Hold the mints above the open bottle in a stack, drop them in all at once, and run away!

3 The cola will explode from the bottle like a geyser, and if you are not quick enough, you will be drenched!

4 Try it with a variety of different diet colas and mints to see which combinations work the best.

WHY DOES IT HAPPEN?

No one really knows! However, it is thought that the mints release substances that change the nature of the cola and accelerate the formation of carbon-dioxide bubbles. This also exposes thousands of tiny pits on the surface of each mint, and these are perfect places for bubbles to form. As the mints sink to the bottom of the bottle, the bubbles blast the cola out at a high velocity, sometimes up to 20 ft (6 m) or more.

4 Experiment with the mixture. If you drop it on the floor, it should bounce, but if you leave it there, it will form a puddle. How weird is that?

Make a flashlight

It's a small but very bright flashlight, it's a key ring, and it's also a fish! To make this flashlight, you can recycle materials—plastic from a milk carton, cardboard from a box, and foil from candy wrappers. You need to buy a light-emitting diode (LED) and a battery. LEDs are used in everything from jumbo jets to TV screens, but they are also bright enough to be used in flashlights.

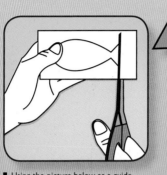

1 Using the picture below as a guide, draw a fish onto the plastic. Mark small notches on both sides of the tail and body and at the tip. Cut the fish shape out.

The center of the hole should be about 1 in (25 mm) from the tip.

2 Do the same for the cardboard layer. Cut a round hole slightly smaller than the battery (os that it will be held tight) and a small notch for the LED to sit in at the tip.

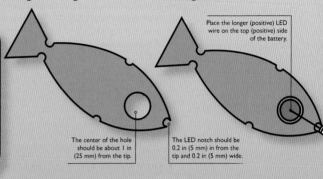

Place the longer (positive) LED wire on the top (positive) side of the battery.

The LED notch should be 0.2 in (5 mm) in from the tip and 0.2 in (5 mm) wide.

3 Slip the battery into the hole and the LED in the notch. Tape the short (negative) LED wire to the back of the battery. Slightly bend the longer LED wire away from the front.

TOP TIP
How about cutting your flashlight into the shape of a lighthouse, a snake, or a pencil and decorating it with foil, candy wrappers, or glitter?

4 Next, decorate the fish, covering the cardboard in colored paper. Add circles for the eyes over the battery.

5 Put the plastic on each side and secure with rubber bands at the notches. Punch a hole in the tail and add the key ring.

Use thin plastic from a drink bottle to protect your flashlight if you keep it in your pocket or with your keys.

Ask your local hardware shop for an LED and battery to suit your flashlight.

Notches hold the rubber bands in place.

6 When you press the eye, the LED turns on. Your fish flashlight is ready to light your world!

Power an electromagnet

An electromagnet is different from a normal magnet because it works only if you run an electric current through it. When you turn off the current, the magnetism is turned off, too, so you can pick something up magnetically and then drop it.

1 Wrap at least 24 in (60 cm) of thin wire tightly around a 4 in (10 cm) steel nail, leaving at least 4 in (10 cm) free at each end.

2 Use tape to connect one free end of the wire to the negative terminal of a 9-volt battery. Touch a paperclip with the nail. Nothing should happen.

3 Tape the other end of the wire to the positive terminal of the battery, and touch the paperclip with the nail again. It should pick it up like a magnet. If you remove the taped wire from the battery, the nail will drop it again.

4 Reattach the wire and move a compass near the nail. The compass needle will respond to the magnetism. Switch the wires on the battery and the needle will swing in the other direction because you've reversed the electromagnet's polarity.

LEVITATION
Maglev (magnetic levitation) trains ride, friction free, on an air cushion created by the magnetic field of electromagnets.

Positive terminal

Negative terminal

Use a lemon as a battery

Batteries consist of two different metals suspended in an acidic solution. Copper from a coin and a zinc nail work well as the metals, and you can use a lemon's acidic juice as the solution. Connect a few together and you can power a light.

You will need:

5 large lemons, 5 copper coins, and 5 zinc-galvanized nails

5 alligator clips

6 lengths of insulated wire

3-volt LED

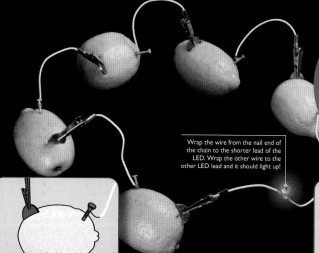

TOP TIP
One lemon generates only about 0.7 volts of electricity, so to get a good result, you will need to link a few lemons together.

Wrap the wire from the nail end of the chain to the shorter lead of the LED. Wrap the other wire to the other LED lead and it should light up!

1 Insert a coin into a cut made on one end of a lemon, and leave it sticking out slightly. Push a galvanized nail into the other end of the lemon. Do the same for four more lemons.

2 Wrap the bare end of one wire around the nail and attach an alligator clip to the other end. Repeat with the other nails, but leave one wire without a clip. Save this for the remaining length of wire.

3 Take the wire from one lemon and clip the free end to a coin in another lemon. Do this in sequence as it appears above. You should have a free lead at each end of the chain.

4 Link the lead from the nail to the negative (short) LED wire, and the lead from the last coin to the positive (long) wire. The LED should light up, giving you a lemon-powered battery!

Launch a bottle rocket

Did you know that you can make a rocket powered by water and air? Okay, it won't reach the stars, but it should soar high up into the air—and since it can't get far, you can easily find it and launch it again!

TOP TIP
Use a soda bottle, because it will usually be made of stronger plastic than a water bottle.

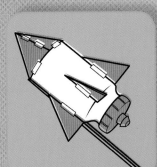

1 Tape the stick to the side of the smaller bottle, with the neck of the bottle facing down. Make a nose cone and fins from cardboard, and tape them to the bottle to make it look the part.

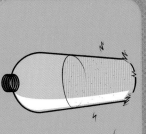

2 Next build your launch pad. Half fill the big soda bottle with sand so that it stands upright and is stable. If it's not, try partially burying the base in the ground.

Launch the rocket in an open area away from buildings and people.

3 Turn the rocket nose down and fill it one third full with water. Screw on the cap. Pull the stopper open and push the conical plastic nozzle of the pump into the hole. It must be a tight fit.

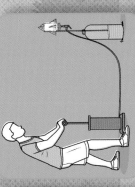

4 Carefully turn your rocket upright and insert the stick into the soda bottle. Start pumping. As you pump, air pressure will build up in the top part of the rocket above the water.

5 Suddenly the air pressure will blow the pump nozzle out of the stopper, and the water will blast out to propel the rocket high up into the air. Stand back or you could get a bit wet.

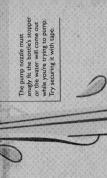

The pump nozzle must snugly fit the bottle's stopper or the water will come out while you're trying to pump. Try securing it with tape.

Be an astronaut

Do you dream of one day traveling into space? Training to be an astronaut takes years of dedication, and first you must get through a killer selection procedure since space agencies take on only a handful of new recruits each year. Here are the key skills you'll need to succeed.

Do you have what it takes?

Applicants are usually in their late 20s or early 30s—this might seem old but it's because you've got a lot of training to do before you can apply.

Health: You need to be healthy, of normal weight, mentally sound, and have excellent eyesight. And you should be about 5 ft 1 in–6 ft 2 in (153–190 cm) tall.

Education: You'll need excellent grades and an advanced degree in a science-based subject for your application to be considered.

Languages: Fluency in English is vital, but a good working knowledge of Russian is also a plus, since many training centers are in Russia.

Flying experience: If you want to be a spacecraft pilot, you'll need to be a qualified jet pilot, preferably with many years in the armed services under your belt.

Personal qualities: Good reasoning capability and memory are key. You'll also need to be highly motivated and emotionally stable to withstand the pressure of the application process, which can take many months, not to mention the stresses of the job itself!

TEAMWORK

Astronauts enjoy the limelight, but they wouldn't get very far without all of the people on Earth supporting them. So if you don't make it as an astronaut, why not join the team as one of the engineers or scientists who build and maintain spacecraft, plan missions, or work at mission control monitoring each space flight and providing guidance from Earth.

Are you sure?

Being an astronaut has its down sides. Before you commit, consider the following:

- You're in for a bumpy ride. About one half of all astronauts suffer from motion sickness in space. Imagine getting travel sick with the added twist of not even knowing which way is up.

- Space food means prepackaged meals—day after day after day. Some foods are dried and must be rehydrated by adding water. Yum.

- You'll be sharing a small space with six other people for long periods. There's no getting away from people in space!

- To stop your muscles wasting away, you'll need to exercise on a treadmill for two hours each day.

- There are no power showers in space. Things—including you—will stink a little bit.

SPACE TOURIST
If you don't make it as an astronaut, for $20–25 million, you could travel to the International Space Station as a space tourist.

Explore the Moon

Seen with the naked eye, the Moon looks like a bright disk, but seen close up, it is clearly a huge ball of rock in the sky. You need a clear, starry night, preferably when it's cold so that there is not much water vapor in the air. The Moon is best viewed on frosty winter nights.

Phases of the Moon

The Moon seems to change shape over a month because the Sun strikes it at different angles. The shape we see changes every day, but only the main phases are named. We see only one side of the Moon because it rotates on its axis at the same rate that it travels around Earth—once every 29.5 days.

1 New Moon
2 Waxing crescent
3 First quarter
4 Waxing gibbous
5 Full Moon
6 Waning gibbous
7 Last quarter
8 Waning crescent
9 New Moon

DARK SIDE

We never see the other "dark" side of the Moon from Earth, but we do have images of it from spacecraft—and it's not always dark!

The side of the Moon facing us is attracted by Earth's gravity because it has more mass than the "dark" side.

Selecting viewing point

Find a place with no trees or bright lights. If you are using binoculars, it's best to rest them on a support such as a tripod (see below).

Using binoculars

Center the binoculars on the Moon, lock the tripod if you are using one, and adjust the focus until you get a crisp image.

Using a telescope

A telescope gives a closer view of the Moon's features. Start with a low magnification and increase it until you have a sharp image.

TOP TIP

Binoculars will give you a 3-D view of the Moon's globe. A telescope will show more detail, but it won't be in 3-D.

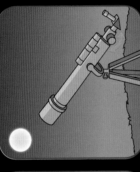

A Full Moon is directly illuminated by the Sun, but it's more impressive to look at when the Sun's light strikes it at an angle.

Moon features

1. Plato (crater)
2. Sea of Showers
3. Montes Caucasus
4. Apollo 15 landing site
5. Sea of Serenity
6. Aristarchus (crater)
7. Montes Apenninus
8. Apollo 17 landing site
9. Montes Carpatus
10. Sea of Tranquility
11. Sea of Crises
12. Kepler (crater)
13. Copernicus (crater)
14. Apollo 11 landing site
15. Sea of Fertility
16. Grimaldi (crater)
17. Apollo 14 landing site
18. Apollo 16 landing site
19. Sea of Clouds
20. Sea of Moisture
21. Sea of Nectar
22. Tycho (crater)

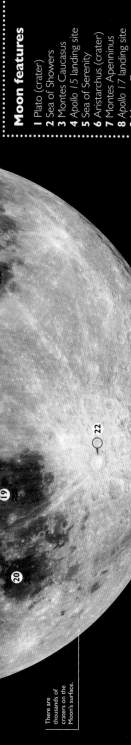

There are thousands of craters on the Moon's surface.

Craters

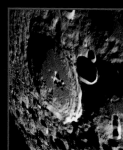

Round craters are made by asteroids hitting the Moon. Rock fragments were blasted across the surface by the impacts.

Maria

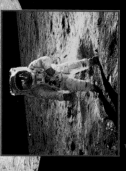

The big dark areas are the maria, or "seas," which were created by vast flows of lava, mostly basalt, about 3.6 billion years ago.

Landing sites

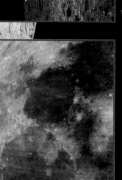

The first people to walk on the Moon were the Apollo 11 astronauts in 1969. They landed in the Sea of Tranquility.

Mountains

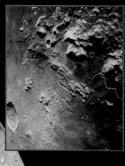

The Moon's lighter regions are mountains (montes) formed by asteroid impacts. They are jagged, tall, and often very steep.

Make a binoculars stand

The 3-D images seen through binoculars are ideal for exploring the surface features of our satellite. By attaching a pair of binoculars to a camera tripod, you have a perfectly steady way to view the Moon.

Important!
Ask an adult to help with the drilling. The wood is best secured in a vise to stop it from moving.

You will need:

Binoculars

Camera tripod

Block of wood

Drill

Strong rubber bands

1 Take a block of wood that is roughly 2 in (5 cm) longer than the width of your binoculars. Make a 0.55 mm/²/₃₂ drill hole roughly in the middle.

Drill a hole in the center.

2 Screw the wood to the tripod head, ensuring that it is steady. Secure the binoculars with two elastic bands. You're ready to Moonwatch!

Adjust the tripod head to point the binoculars at the Moon and lock.

Use strong elastic bands to hold the binoculars in place.

Turn the focusing wheel until you have a sharp image.

Don't touch the focusing wheel with the bands.

Extend the tripod legs to full length.

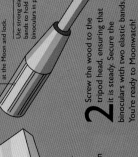

Find constellations

To find their way around the night sky, stargazers over the centuries have grouped the brightest stars into patterns called constellations. There are 88 in total, and each one is named after a person, creature, or object. Here are two to look out for.

Although the stars in a constellation look close together, they are actually completely unrelated and at vastly differing distances from Earth.

Orion
Look for Orion, the Hunter, in the winter in the Northern Hemisphere and in the summer in the south. First, find the red star Betelgeuse at his shoulder, and then the blue star Rigel at bottom right.

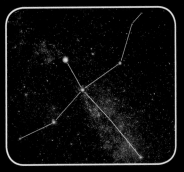

Cygnus
A prominent constellation in the northern fall and southern spring is Cygnus, the Swan, with its long neck and wings and short tail (top left) marked by the bright star Deneb.

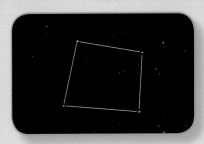

Asterisms
You might find it easier to identify an asterism—a part of a constellation that is easily recognizable. For example, the four stars that make up a square shape in the constellation of Pegasus are easier to recognize than the full constellation.

Make an eclipse viewer

Sometimes, the Moon moves in front of the sun and blocks out its light, either partially or totally, in a solar eclipse. It's a spectacular event, but you can't watch it directly because sunlight—even eclipsed—would blind you. So what should you do? When an eclipse is predicted, get ready by making a simple eclipse viewer.

You will need:

Two sheets of thin white cardboard

Sharp pencil or pointed instrument

1 Punch a small hole about the size of a pencil point in the middle of a sheet of white cardboard. When the Moon starts moving across the sun, turn your back to the sun and hold up the sheet so that the sun is shining through the hole.

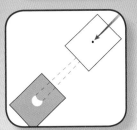

2 Hold a second sheet of cardboard in the shadow of the first, about 2 ft (50 cm) away. The pinhole will act like a lens and project an image of the eclipsed sun onto the second sheet.

The image of the eclipse is projected onto the cardboard.

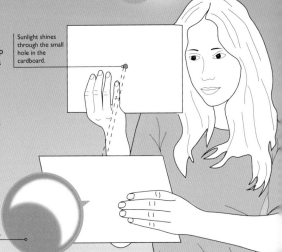

3 Move the sheets closer to each other to get a smaller, sharper image. You will see the bright crescent get smaller and then bigger again as the Moon moves across the sun.

Sunlight shines through the small hole in the cardboard.

Get a comet named after you

While the planets follow roughly circular orbits around the Sun, other objects called comets loop close to the Sun, releasing tails of gas and dust, and then hurtle off into the distant solar system. If you spot a new comet it is named after you.

1 Scan the skies! A telescope is the best instrument. As you search, note exactly where you are looking, with reference to the stars of a nearby constellation.

2 If you do spot something, check online for lists of known comets—it is likely to be a comet that someone has already spotted before.

3 If you don't see your comet anywhere, the next step is to let the Central Bureau for Astronomical Telegrams (CBAT) know. They are the official body that deals with comets.

4 If it is truly a new comet, congratulations! The comet will be named after you, but if it is discovered by more than one person at the same time, the comet will be named after both discoverers.

Bright comets

Here are three recent bright comet discoveries:

Hale-Bopp (see above) Discovered by Alan Hale and Thomas Bopp in 1995.

Hyakutake Discovered by amateur astronomer Yuji Hyakutake in 1996.

McNaught Discovered by Robert H. McNaught in 2007.

Moon

Venus

Mars

See planets

The four brightest planets—Venus, Mars, Jupiter, and Saturn—can be seen at night among the stars. Check online for where they are in the sky based on your location and date, but read these tips first.

Use stars to guide your way on pages 124–125.

Venus
The easiest planet to see with the naked eye, Venus is the brightest object in the night sky and can sometimes be seen in daylight when clear of the Sun. It appears bright white and is best observed in the western sky after sunset.

Mars
From Earth, you can see this rocky planet's orange-red color caused by the rusty iron in its rocks and sand. Features such as the polar icecaps and dried-up water channels can be seen with a powerful telescope.

Jupiter
This is the most obvious planet in the sky—a clear white disk rather than a twinkling pinpoint of light. Using binoculars or a small telescope, find four of the planet's moons—Europa, Ganymede, Io, and Callisto—nearby.

Saturn
To the naked eye, this planet looks pale yellow in the night sky. Unless you have a very good telescope, its famous rings won't be visible. You may be able to see its elliptical shape through binoculars.

SURVIVE IN THE WILD

If you're planning an expedition in the big outdoors, it's important to be prepared and master some basic survival skills before you set off. Discover how to find your way, build a shelter, catch fish, avoid a bear, and—at the end of the day—make a glowing campfire to cook on or just sit around.

Avoid getting lost

Some people get lost easily. Don't be one of them! If you are going anywhere unfamiliar, arm yourself with a map so that you can find out where you are. This is especially useful in a city, where you can simply look up a street name. If you are in the country and don't have a map, there are still things you can do to keep yourself out of trouble and find your way back to where you started.

Stay aware of the Sun's position by watching the shadows. The Sun is a good indicator of direction.

Safety!

If you are heading off into the wilderness, take a phone, and make sure someone knows where you are going and when you plan to return.

Look and learn. Observe the lie of the land and note obvious features such as streams and rocks.

Don't just look ahead; look back, too. If you are returning by the same route, note how it will look.

Make a habit of using your compass at regular intervals from the start of the walk.

Don't just follow someone else. If he or she loses their way, you will both be lost.

Advice

• Be extra careful at all intersections and try to form a mental picture of the landscape and how it might look from the air, with you walking through it.

• Take a compass with you and learn how to use it—know at least enough to tell which way is north. You might be surprised at how useful it can be.

• If you are out with friends, it is easy to fall deep into a conversation and lose track of where you are. This is one of the main reasons people get lost, so be wary of this when traveling in a group.

• If you do get lost, stop moving, stay calm, and formulate a plan. Wandering off in any direction not only doesn't help you, but it could also increase the distance that a search party may have to cover.

Make a shadow compass

As the Earth turns, shadows move across the ground from west to east. You can use this fact to figure out the direction of east, west, north, and south. The technique works best near the equator, but you can try it anywhere—provided it's a sunny day!

1 Push a stick into flat ground or find something that will do the same job, such as a fence post. Wait until you can see a strong shadow, then mark the end of the shadow with a distinctive stone or some other conspicuous object.

2 Wait at least 15 minutes, until the end of the shadow has moved some distance across the ground. Then mark the end of the shadow with another stone. The longer you wait, the more accurate your compass will be.

3 Using a stick, draw a straight line on the ground between the two stones. This indicates east and west, with the first stone marking west. You can then add another line at right angles to indicate north and south.

Watch your way

If you are in the midlatitudes—that is, between the Tropics and the polar regions—you can use an ordinary wristwatch to find north and south. The technique is different depending on whether you are north or south of the equator.

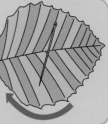

North of the equator
Hold your watch flat and turn it so that the hour hand points at the Sun. Find the point halfway between the hour hand and the 12 o'clock mark on the watch. This halfway position will be pointing south.

South of the equator
Turn your watch so that the 12 o'clock mark points at the Sun. Then find the halfway point between the 12 o'clock mark and the hour hand. This halfway position indicates where north is.

Improvise a magnet compass

A compass needle is just a small light magnet on a pivot that responds to the Earth's magnetic field by aligning itself with north and south. You can make your own compass by using water to support a free-floating magnetized needle.

You will need:

Small magnet

Steel needle

Puddle or bowl of water

Leaf

Get fancy with an electromagnet on page 173.

TOP TIP
If you don't have a magnet, try stroking the needle with a piece of fabric such as silk. This may have the same effect.

1 First, magnetize your needle. Stroke it from the middle to the point about 20 times with one end of the magnet, then stroke it from the middle to the eye with the other end of the magnet.

2 Place the leaf on the surface of the water and carefully lay the needle on top. Because they are floating freely, the needle and leaf will automatically rotate to align with north and south.

3 Double-check against the Sun. The end that points toward it at noon should point south if you are in the Northern Hemisphere, and north if you are in the Southern Hemisphere.

Steer by the stars

For centuries, sailors navigated the oceans using the positions of the stars by night and the Sun by day. Modern sailors use more sophisticated methods such as GPS (Global Positioning System) devices to find their exact position, but if you are out in the wilderness, you can still use the Sun and stars to find your way.

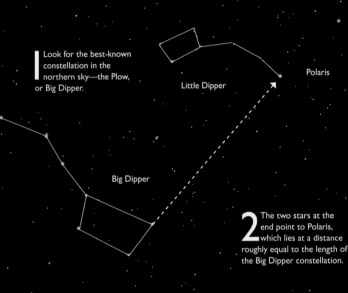

1 Look for the best-known constellation in the northern sky—the Plow, or Big Dipper.

Little Dipper

Big Dipper

Polaris

2 The two stars at the end point to Polaris, which lies at a distance roughly equal to the length of the Big Dipper constellation.

North Star

In the Northern Hemisphere, you can find north by locating the North Star, Polaris. Most stars in the sky appear to move as Earth spins on its axis, but since Polaris is almost directly above the North Pole, it hardly moves at all.

Find your latitude

The latitude of a place on the globe is its distance north or south of the equator. If you're in the Northern Hemisphere, you can use Polaris and an inclinometer, a device to measure angles, to figure out your latitude, and how close to the equator you are.

1 Carefully copy this image onto a sheet of stiff card and tie a weight or a small key to a length of string, and attach it to the corner.

2 Point the inclinometer toward Polaris. The string will hang at a position relative to your latitude on the globe.

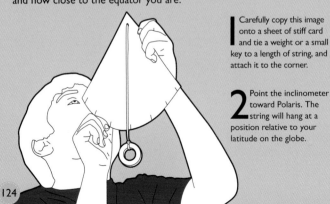

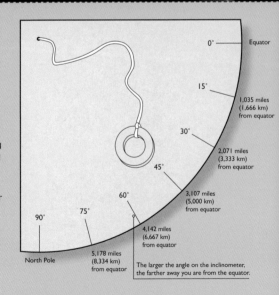

0° — Equator

15°
1,035 miles (1,666 km) from equator

30°
2,071 miles (3,333 km) from equator

45°
3,107 miles (5,000 km) from equator

60°
4,142 miles (6,667 km) from equator

75°
5,178 miles (8,334 km) from equator

90°
North Pole

The larger the angle on the inclinometer, the farther away you are from the equator.

Southern Cross

In the Southern Hemisphere, there is no conspicuous star that stays conveniently over the South Pole, so locating south is a little trickier.

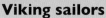

Viking sailors

Long ago, the Vikings sailed regularly from Norway to their settlements on the southern tip of Greenland by using the height of the midday Sun above the horizon to judge their latitude (distance from the equator).

Southern Cross

Pointers

Southern Celestial Pole

South Pole

1 Find the Southern Cross—a compact group of bright stars with two nearby stars pointing to them.

2 Imagine extending the main axis of the cross in the direction of the brightest star. Do this again from halfway between the pointers.

3 The South Pole lies below the point where the two imaginary lines meet.

Locate north and south

If you know the time, you can use the Sun's position to find north and south. At noon, when the Sun is at its highest point, the shadows cast will be shortest and will point due north if you are in the Southern Hemisphere and due south if you are in the Northern Hemisphere.

1 Around noon, push a stick into the ground and watch its shadow change from long to short. When the shadow is shortest, the Sun is at its highest point.

2 This shortest shadow cast by the Sun will point toward the North Pole in the Northern Hemisphere and the South Pole in the Southern Hemisphere.

Geocaching

If you enjoy a treasure hunt, you'll like geocaching. It's an organized activity using a GPS device to seek out "caches"—things hidden by other players around the world and can be combined with a hike or a camping trip. Find out more online.

Hike safely in bear country

Hiking with friends is a great way to enjoy nature, but when traveling through wild areas where bears live you must take precautions.

Store food away from your tent, sealing it in plastic bags and hanging them from a high clothesline between trees.

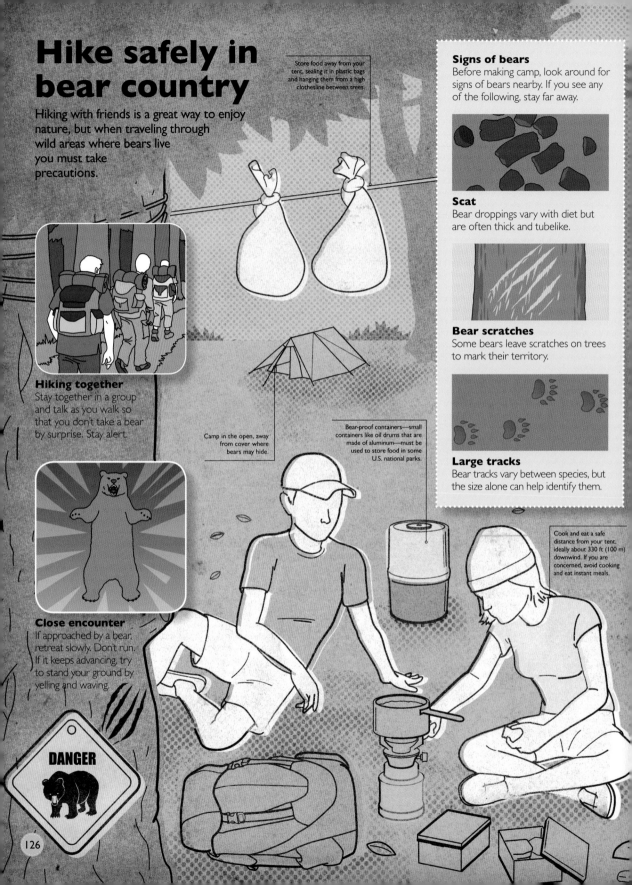

Hiking together
Stay together in a group and talk as you walk so that you don't take a bear by surprise. Stay alert.

Camp in the open, away from cover where bears may hide.

Bear-proof containers—small containers like oil drums that are made of aluminum—must be used to store food in some U.S. national parks.

Close encounter
If approached by a bear, retreat slowly. Don't run. If it keeps advancing, try to stand your ground by yelling and waving.

Cook and eat a safe distance from your tent, ideally about 330 ft (100 m) downwind. If you are concerned, avoid cooking and eat instant meals.

DANGER

Signs of bears
Before making camp, look around for signs of bears nearby. If you see any of the following, stay far away.

Scat
Bear droppings vary with diet but are often thick and tubelike.

Bear scratches
Some bears leave scratches on trees to mark their territory.

Large tracks
Bear tracks vary between species, but the size alone can help identify them.

Escape an alligator

If you come face to face with an alligator, run away fast. If this is not an option and you are attacked, fight back. An alligator prefers an easy meal, and it may give up and release you.

Dos and don'ts
• Never feed alligators, deliberately, or accidentally, by leaving food around. It encourages them to become bolder near people.

• Watch where you walk. Stay away from the water's edge, especially at night. Be sure to avoid thick vegetation where alligators may lurk.

• Look out for sliding marks where alligators enter the water, and if you spot them, avoid the area.

Flee
Run away in a straight line. It's a myth that you should flee from an alligator in a zigzag pattern.

Wrestle
Try to get behind the animal to avoid its mouth. If bitten, don't thrash around but punch its snout hard.

Avoid a shark attack

Shark attacks are rare. There were only an estimated 59 attacks worldwide in 2008, most off the coast of Florida. Nevertheless, it's important to take precautions.

Dos and don'ts
• In areas known to be shark territory, don't go into the water alone, especially at night.

• If you must swim or surf in a shark habitat, wear a wetsuit since sharks don't like rubber.

• Never go into dangerous water if you are bleeding, even if it's a small cut. Sharks can smell a drop of blood from a long distance.

• If there is a shark alert, leave the water quickly but calmly, with minimum fuss.

Avoid dark, murky water since sharks have poor vision and may mistake you for their normal prey.

Punch on the nose
If seized, try to keep your back to the shark. Punch its nose and eyes and shout for help.

Avoid bites and stings

The most dangerous animals are not giant sharks, bears, or crocodiles but are much smaller creatures that bite, sting, or transmit nasty diseases. They include venomous snakes, scorpions, and a variety of flies and other insects. You will need to know how to avoid these—and what to do if you fail.

Mosquitoes

Danger
Millions of people suffer from diseases carried by tropical mosquitoes. These include yellow fever, the West Nile virus, dengue, and especially malaria, which kills up to three million people per year. Some people are also allergic to mosquito bites.

Advice
In the Tropics, use insect repellent on your skin and always sleep under a mosquito net. You can also get mosquito-repellent candles and other devices.

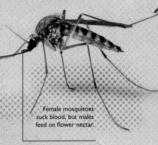

Female mosquitoes suck blood, but males feed on flower nectar.

Ticks and mites

Danger
These tiny bloodsucking relatives of spiders live in swamps and forests. Mites cause itchy rashes, but the slightly larger ticks may carry deadly diseases that attack the brain.

Advice
Deter them by wearing long pants tucked into socks. If you find a tick attached to your skin, grip its head end with tweezers and carefully pull it out, then take it with you to the doctor.

The body of this tick is swollen to the size of a pea with its victim's blood.

A scorpion has a sharp stinger on the end of its long, flexible tail.

Scorpions

Danger
These spider relatives live in the hotter parts of the world. Their stings can be very dangerous and cause thousands of deaths each year.

Advice
Scorpions creep into dark crevices, so carefully check clothes and footwear—and turn over rocks with caution.

Spiders

Danger
All spiders are venomous. Luckily, very few are able to bite humans, but some spiders are very dangerous. They include the Brazilian wandering spider, American black widow (above), Australian redback, and Australian funnel-web spider.

Advice
If you are bitten by any of these spiders, you need medical attention fast. Don't risk it! Avoid places where they might live and carefully check clothing and footwear.

Ants, wasps, and bees

Danger
Many of these live in large colonies, which they defend by swarming over intruders and biting or stinging them.

Advice
Stay away from nests or beehives. Get medical help fast if you suffer multiple stings or if any stings are inside your nose, mouth, or throat. If you are stung by a bee, remove the stinger by pulling it out with your fingers.

Safety!
If you feel sick after being bitten or stung, get medical help. Try to describe what attacked you so that the doctor knows exactly how to treat it.

ANAPHYLAXIS

A bee or wasp sting is usually just painful, but some people suffer a very dangerous allergic reaction called anaphylaxis. If a friend is stung and starts to suffer faintness, nausea, and has difficulty breathing, get emergency medical help. The cure is an adrenaline injection, and people who know they are allergic may carry adrenaline just in case. Check for this and use it. You could save a life.

Identify deadly snakes

Most snakes are not venomous at all, but some can be deadly. The snakes shown here are some of the most dangerous, either because of the power of their venom or because they hide in places where they are easy to step on. Even so, most of them will bite only in self-defense.

Rattlesnake
Several types of rattlesnakes live in the hotter, drier parts of the U.S. They threaten enemies by rattling the loose scales on their tails.

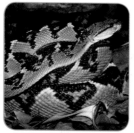

Bushmaster
This is the biggest venomous snake in the Americas. It lives in tropical forests, where it lies concealed among the dead leaves, so it is easy to step on by mistake.

Black mamba
An African relative of the cobra, this is one of the quickest of all venomous snakes, moving as fast as a person can run. It can grow to more than 13 ft (4 m) long!

Russell's viper
This Asian viper kills thousands of people every year in rural India, mostly because of its habit of lurking on paths near villages.

Gaboon viper
This African ambush hunter uses its superb camouflage to hide among leaves. It has the longest fangs of any venomous snake.

Indian cobra
The cobra is notorious for the way in which it rears up and spreads its broad "hood" in a threat display, as well as for its deadly venom.

Common krait
This is one of the most venomous snakes in India, but luckily it hunts at night when most people are safely asleep at home.

Inland taipan
This rare Australian snake has the most poisonous venom of all snakes, up to 400 times more toxic than most rattlesnakes!

Death adder
Well named, this Australian ambush hunter has the fastest strike of any snake in the world, as well as highly toxic venom.

Deal with snakebites

Venomous snakes will usually try to escape rather than look for trouble. Most snakebite victims have either stepped on a snake by accident or are trying to catch one or annoy it. So watch where you put your feet, and if you see a snake, leave it alone!

Dos
- When in snake country, wear sturdy boots and consider using a stick to tap the ground in front of you.
- If you or a friend are bitten, stay calm and call for emergency medical help on your cell phone.
- Try to remember what the snake looked like—it could help the doctor a lot. Even better, try to take a photo of it.
- Follow any instructions that the medical team gives you over the phone.
- Remove constricting items such as rings from the bitten area, which may swell up.
- Keep the affected area below the level of the patient's heart. This reduces the flow of venom through the body.
- If the patient is weak and pale, lay him or her flat, but keep the affected area below heart level.

Don'ts
- Don't attempt to suck out the venom.
- Don't cut the wound.
- Don't try to apply a tourniquet.
- If you are trying to identify the snake, be very careful. Don't risk another bite!

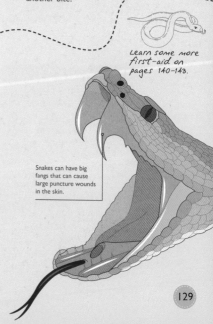

Learn some more first-aid on pages 140–143.

Snakes can have big fangs that can cause large puncture wounds in the skin.

Cross a swamp

Swamps, marshes, and bogs are treacherous wetlands that most people try to avoid crossing. Sometimes, however, you have no choice but to cross a stretch of very wet ground with visible standing water and liquid mud. This is how you might be able to do it.

Use your stick for support and to test the firmness of the ground.

Look out for rocks and stony patches as well as plant clumps to stand on.

If you start sinking, move on until you reach a safe place to stop.

Pick a safe route

• It's useful to have a stick to probe the ground and keep you upright. If you don't have one already, try to find one. Any stick will do, provided it is long enough and has the strength to support your weight.

• Survey the area you want to cross, looking for clumps of grass or similar vegetation. Most plants don't like growing in waterlogged ground, so they mark the drier areas. Their roots also reinforce the soft, wet ground.

• Plan a route that will let you move from one clump of vegetation to the next, with no big gaps. You want to be able to step from point to point without jumping, because you could easily slip and fall if you jump.

• Step onto the nearest clump and stand on it with both feet in order to spread your weight. Then step onto the next clump, then the next, and so on. Keep moving, but make sure you know how to get back if you need to.

Get out of quicksand

Quicksand has a bad reputation for trapping people who then disappear without a trace. In reality, this is unlikely, but getting stuck in quicksand is certainly something you want to avoid. Unfortunately, that is not easy, because quicksand looks just like any other stretch of sand—until you step on it!

WHAT IS QUICKSAND?

Quicksand is a mixture of sand, clay, and salty water that is normally a semisolid gelatin. When the mixture is disturbed—maybe by you stepping on it—the water liquefies the clay so the sand particles easily slip past one another, allowing heavy objects to sink through them.

1 The more you struggle, the faster you will sink. If you relax, your body floats because it is not as dense as the quicksand. So stop struggling and stay calm. This way, you won't drown!

2 Get rid of any heavy equipment. When you've gotten your breath back, work your upper body into a horizontal position to spread your weight on the sand surface and allow you to free your legs.

3 With your body flat on the surface, free one leg at a time from the wet sand. Then lie on your stomach and crawl over the surface to safety, spreading your weight as much as possible.

You will need:

Wooden poles:
- 2 thick poles 12 ft (3.5 m) long
- 2 thick poles 8 ft (2.4 m) long
- 16 thinner poles 8 ft (2.4 m) long

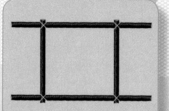

Knife

Strong twine

Extra buoyancy devices

Paddle or long pole

Build a raft

If you need a boat to cross a stretch of water, the simplest solution is to build a raft. You can make one out of anything that floats, such as light, buoyant timber.

TOP TIP
Use a long pole to propel the raft because it will be much more efficient than a paddle.

1 Lay the two long poles on the ground and place the shorter, thick poles on top of them to make a rough square. Use the twine to tie them together.

2 Set six of the thinner poles aside, and tie the others to the frame inside the square to make a platform. Add more poles if necessary to fill any gaps.

3 Tie three of the remaining poles to the protruding ends of the frame at one side to make a stabilizing outrigger. Do the same on the other side.

4 If you have any extra buoyancy devices such as airtight containers, attach these to the undersides of the outriggers. Make sure the buoyancy is balanced.

5 Launch your raft in shallow water and see how it floats with you onboard. If all seems well, you can push off for the far shore.

Empty water bottles with their caps screwed on make good buoyancy tanks.

Stay afloat

Even if you can swim well, it's useful to be able to stay afloat without using much energy. If you can't swim, don't panic! Your body floats naturally—you just need to rest in a way that allows you to breathe.

Go to pages 176-177 to learn how to sail.

Dead man's float

1 Hold your breath and flop forward with your face in the water, your arms out, and your legs dangling.

2 When you need to breathe, paddle your arms up and down, gently kick your feet and raise your head.

Improvised float

1 If you're wearing jeans with a belt, pull them off, tie the legs together, and fill them with air.

2 Pull the belt tight. Then put the jeans over your head, with the waist area in front of you.

131

Treat hypothermia

If someone gets cold enough, their body temperature can drop to a dangerously low level. This is called hypothermia. Someone with severe hypothermia may even stop feeling cold. If this happens, you need to act fast.

1 Usually the victim will be violently shivering. If she suddenly stops shivering, she is seriously hypothermic.

2 Telephone for medical help and quickly get her to a shelter. Remove any wet outer clothing.

3 Wrap the patient up in something warm and dry, such as a dry coat or a sleeping bag.

4 The more layers you use, the better. Giving her a hot drink can also help.

5 Hug her in 15-minute stretches to pass on some of your body heat. Wait for help to arrive.

Survive an avalanche

Avalanches pose a deadly danger in snowy mountain regions. During an avalanche, a huge weight of snow cascades off a mountain slope and collects in a deep solid mass. Caught up in one, you must do all you can to avoid being buried.

Safety! The only sure way to survive an avalanche is to avoid one altogether. If you are ever in a place where an avalanche could occur, be aware of your surroundings and pay attention to warning signs.

1 Turn away from the avalanche and try to keep your back to it. Yell to alert other people and let them know where you are.

2 Get rid of any cumbersome items such as your backpack and skis, because they will only weigh you down.

3 If possible, grab a tree or large rock. The more snow that passes you, the less there is to bury you. Hang on for as long as you can.

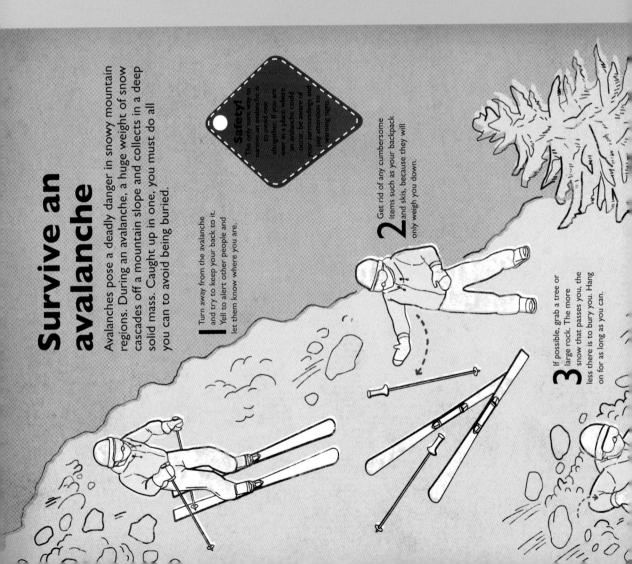

Dig a snow cave

If you are forced to spend the night out in the snow, you could easily freeze to death, but you can survive by digging an emergency shelter in a deep, firm snowdrift.

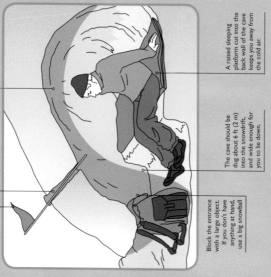

A flag can help rescuers find you. A colorful scarf tied to a stick works just as well.

Leaving a ventilation hole is vital, but don't build it above the sleeping platform.

A domed ceiling means that melting snow will drip down the sides of the cave and not on your head.

A raised sleeping platform cut into the back wall of the cave keeps you away from the cold air.

The cave should be dug about 6 ft (2 m) into the snowdrift, and wide enough for you to lie down.

Block the entrance with a large object. If you don't have anything at hand, use a big snowball.

INSULATION

A snow cave doesn't sound like a very warm prospect, but it can be toastier than a tent if you get it right. The snow insulates you from the freezing night air and prevents the wind from getting in. Building the sleeping platform higher than the entrance is vital—the warm air rises around you and the cold air sinks.

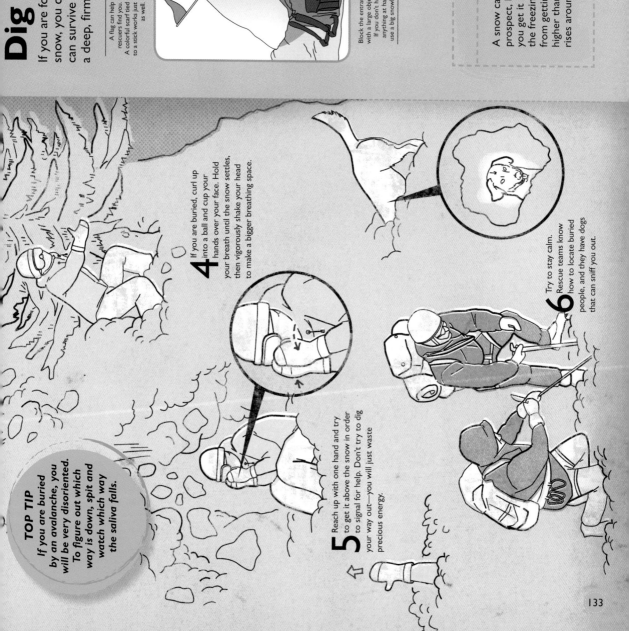

TOP TIP
If you are buried by an avalanche, you will be very disoriented. To figure out which way is down, spit and watch which way the saliva falls.

4 If you are buried, curl up into a ball and cup your hands over your face. Hold your breath until the snow settles, then vigorously shake your head to make a bigger breathing space.

5 Reach up with one hand and try to get it above the snow in order to signal for help. Don't try to dig your way out—you will just waste precious energy.

6 Try to stay calm. Rescue teams know how to locate buried people, and they have dogs that can sniff you out.

Build an igloo

An igloo is a snow shelter built by traditional Arctic hunters who have to spend the night away from home. You can build one yourself if you live in a region that gets deep winter snow. But it takes time, so make sure you're warmly dressed.

The right kind of snow
For the best building blocks, the snow must be just right, not too loose and soft or the blocks will fall apart and not too dense and hard so that they are difficult to cut.

A tunnel helps keep the wind out and the heat in.

1 Find some hard-packed snow at least 4 ft (1.2 m) deep, and use the saw to cut some large rectangular snow blocks—as big as you can carry.

2 Place the blocks in a circle about 8 ft (2.5 m) across, shaping them with the saw or knife so that they butt together. Trim the tops of the blocks so that they slope inward a little.

3 Use the shovel to dig out most of the area inside the circle to 3 ft (1 m) or so below snow level. Leave a raised section at the back of the igloo.

4 Cut more blocks and place them on top of the first layer. Shape them as before and place them across the joins between the blocks below, like bricks in a wall.

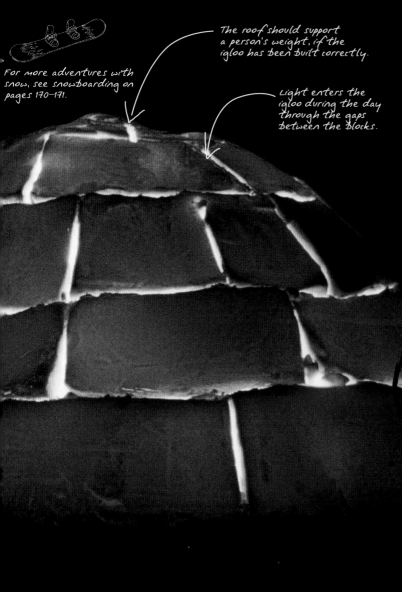

For more adventures with snow, see snowboarding on pages 170–171.

The roof should support a person's weight, if the igloo has been built correctly.

Light enters the igloo during the day through the gaps between the blocks.

For more adventures with snow, see snowboarding on pages 170–171.

THE BIG CHILL

Snow is a good insulator. In the Arctic, the temperature can fall to a bone-chilling –49°F (–45°C), while inside an igloo it could be a milder 19°F (–7°C). Body heat may also melt the inner surface of the walls, which then refreezes to help seal in the warmth.

Living quarters

Inside, the floor of the igloo should be dug out about 3 ft (1 m) below the snow level, leaving a raised sleeping platform at the back. The cold air sinks and gathers in the lower area around the entrance, while the warmer air rises.

5 Cut an arched entrance on one side of the igloo and dig an entrance passage so that you can get in and out. Build a tunnel over the entranceway.

6 Add more layers to the igloo, with each one leaning farther in so that they form a tall dome. To add the final central block, stand inside on any spare snow blocks you have.

7 Plug any gaps with snow, but be sure to leave or make some small holes in the roof for ventilation—it's very important that you have a reliable supply of fresh air.

8 Smooth the inside of the igloo so that any meltwater runs down the walls instead of dripping on you. Then make yourself a warm drink!

Make a simple shelter

If you have to spend a night out in the wilderness, you will want to build some type of shelter from the weather. This will also make you feel much safer from whatever may be out there.

CHOOSE YOUR SITE

Don't just camp anywhere. You need to check out the terrain. Staying near a source of water is useful, but don't camp in a dry riverbed. Heavy rains can transform it into a torrent that could sweep you away. Avoid hazards such as dead trees and branches that could fall on you or rocks from crumbling cliffs. If you have survived an accident involving a conspicuous vehicle, camp nearby, because any rescuers will be looking for it.

Basic tarp tent

If you have a tarpaulin, or any waterproof sheet, you can improvise a shelter by tying a rope between two trees and tossing the tarp over it. Anchor the sides with tent pegs, sharp sticks, or even heavy rocks.

A 6.5 x 10 ft (2 x 3 m) tent flysheet makes a good tarp tent.

Push wire pegs through the eyelets or attach them to extra ropes.

Swing in a hammock

Hammocks are perfect for relaxing and sleeping in. Mexican-style, without stiff spreader bars, are best.

Getting in

Stand with your back to the hammock, sit down, lie back, and swing up.

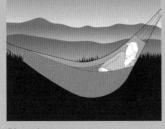

Sleeping

Lie diagonally, not end to end, so that the hammock supports your back.

Tarp and hammock combo

This arrangement is ideal for a hot, wet climate where you want plenty of ventilation but need to stay clear of damp ground. Attach long guy ropes to the eyelets of the tarp or flysheet so that you can stretch it over your hammock.

You can make simple tent pegs from sticks.

TOP TIP
If you are able to carry a lightweight waterproof sheet, you can stay warm and dry.

Build a cozy bivouac

In a cold climate, you'll need a much warmer shelter than a simple tarp tent. You can build one quite easily using branches, leaves, and brushwood. Make it as small as possible so that your body heat warms up the air inside.

1 Wedge a forked branch in the ground and place a long, sturdy pole in the fork, with the other end in the ground. Check that it is long enough to sleep under, with about 2 ft (60 cm) to spare.

2 Create an A-frame for the tent door by resting sturdy diagonal poles opposite each other that meet at the fork. If necessary, use twine or plant stems to tie the main frame together.

3 Lean short poles against the ridge, checking that you have room to lie down inside and turn over in your sleep. Be sure they don't protrude more than 1.5 in (4 cm) above the ridge pole.

4 If you have a sheet, drape it over the top and hold it down with rocks or sharp sticks. If not, cover the timber with a thick layer of leaves arranged like roof tiles so that they repel any rain.

Simple lean-to

A simple lean-to facing a campfire is another practical structure. Push two forked branches into the ground and rest a long pole in the forks. Lean more poles from the ground to the ridge pole and cover these with a roof made of leaves layered like roof tiles.

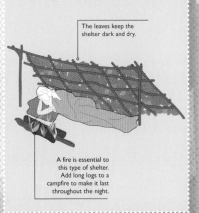

The leaves keep the shelter dark and dry.

A fire is essential to this type of shelter. Add long logs to a campfire to make it last throughout the night.

5 Hold the leaves down with a covering of thin brushwood. Pile dry grass or pine needles inside the shelter to insulate you from the ground. Then slide in and block the entrance.

In freezing weather, pour water on the roof to create an insulating layer of ice.

Make sure you leave some ventilation gaps when you block the entrance.

Survive in the desert

Deserts are not always hot, especially at night, but all deserts are extremely dry, and this is what makes them dangerous. If you are out in the desert, you must take care not to lose too much body moisture, and you will need to either carry or find enough water to stay hydrated.

Avoid losing moisture

If you can cut down the amount of water your body loses, you won't need to drink as much. Move slowly to reduce perspiration and avoid traveling in the heat of the day. Don't reveal too much bare skin—this just allows sweat to evaporate more easily.

Safety!
You should never go out into the desert unless you are carrying enough water. You need at least 2 quarts (2 liters) per person per day.

Wear light clothing and cover your face with a scarf to stop sunburn.

When the sun is high up in the sky, try to find some shade. Rest there, moving as little as possible until the temperature drops.

You will need:

Shovel

Small container

Plastic tube

Clear plastic sheet

Rocks

Collect evaporating ground water

If digging a hole doesn't work, you can collect water vapor rising from damp ground and turn into water. It is a slow process, though, so it is worth trying only as a last resort. Do the job in the early morning, because you need the heat of the sun to evaporate the water.

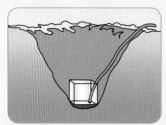

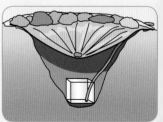

1 Locate a site that is damp beneath the surface but that is in full sunlight. Dig a hole about 24 in (60 cm) deep and wide. Place the container in the hole and put one end of the tube in it. Drag the other end out of the hole.

2 Cover the hole with the plastic sheet, holding down the edges with a ring of rocks so that it lies flat. Add some of the soil or sand from the hole to the ring of rocks. This will weigh down the sheet and seal it to the ground surface.

3 Place a rock in the center of the sheet so that it forms a depression directly above the container. Wait. Eventually you will see moisture collecting on the sheet, running toward the middle and dripping into the container.

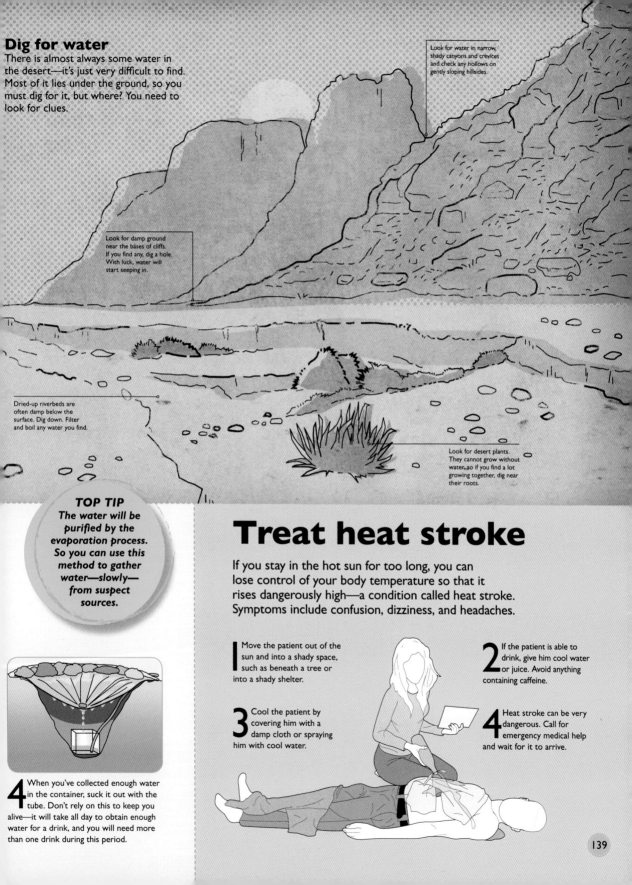

Dig for water

There is almost always some water in the desert—it's just very difficult to find. Most of it lies under the ground, so you must dig for it, but where? You need to look for clues.

Look for water in narrow, shady canyons and crevices and check any hollows on gently sloping hillsides.

Look for damp ground near the bases of cliffs. If you find any, dig a hole. With luck, water will start seeping in.

Dried-up riverbeds are often damp below the surface. Dig down. Filter and boil any water you find.

Look for desert plants. They cannot grow without water, so if you find a lot growing together, dig near their roots.

TOP TIP
The water will be purified by the evaporation process. So you can use this method to gather water—slowly—from suspect sources.

4 When you've collected enough water in the container, suck it out with the tube. Don't rely on this to keep you alive—it will take all day to obtain enough water for a drink, and you will need more than one drink during this period.

Treat heat stroke

If you stay in the hot sun for too long, you can lose control of your body temperature so that it rises dangerously high—a condition called heat stroke. Symptoms include confusion, dizziness, and headaches.

1 Move the patient out of the sun and into a shady space, such as beneath a tree or into a shady shelter.

2 If the patient is able to drink, give him cool water or juice. Avoid anything containing caffeine.

3 Cool the patient by covering him with a damp cloth or spraying him with cool water.

4 Heat stroke can be very dangerous. Call for emergency medical help and wait for it to arrive.

Perform CPR

If someone's heart stops and they stop breathing, the lack of oxygen makes the brain start dying within minutes. Open the airway and check to see if they are breathing. Put your cheek over their mouth and nose, looking to see if the chest is rising and falling. If they are not breathing, you will need to perform cardiopulmonary resuscitation (CPR) until help arrives.

Open the airway

This vital procedure is very easy to do. Place one hand on the casualty's forehead and gently tilt the head back, then lift the chin using only two fingers. This will move the casualty's tongue away from the back of the mouth.

Adult casualty

Immediately call an ambulance, unless the casualty is unconscious from drowning—in which case you should give five initial rescue breaths and perform the following CPR sequence for one minute before making the call. But if anyone else nearby can call an ambulance earlier, get them to do so.

Give 30 chest compressions

1 Place the heel of one hand in the center of the casualty's chest. Then put your other hand on top of the first and interlock the fingers, curling the top fingers under.

2 Raise your fingers and, keeping your arms straight, press down by 2 in (5 cm). Then release the pressure, keeping your hands in place. Repeat this 30 times in 20 seconds.

Give two rescue breaths

3 Ensure that the airway is open (see above). Firmly pinch the nose closed, take a deep breath, seal your lips around the casualty's mouth, and blow into it until the chest rises.

Child casualty

If you are alone and the casualty is a child aged between one and about 14 years old, carry out rescue breaths and chest compressions for one minute before calling an ambulance. If you have someone with you who can help, get them to call an ambulance.

Give five rescue breaths

1 Ensure that the airway is open by tilting the head back and lifting the chin (see above). Then seal your lips around the child's mouth while pinching the nostrils closed.

2 Blow gently into the lungs while looking along the chest. Do not completely empty your lungs. As the chest rises, stop blowing and allow it to fall. Repeat four more times.

Give 30 chest compressions

3 Depending on the child's size, place the heel of one or two hands in the center of the chest. Holding your arm(s) straight, press down to one third of the depth of the chest.

The recovery position

An unconscious casualty who is breathing and has no other life-threatening conditions should be placed in the recovery position.

Turn the casualty onto her side.

Pull the outer leg forward and bend it so the patient cannot roll over.

Continuously monitor breathing and pulse.

Lift her chin forward to open her airway. Adjust her hand under her cheek as necessary.

If her injuries allow, turn the casualty on her other side after 30 minutes.

4 Pull away and allow the chest to fall. Repeat, then perform 30 more compressions. Continue until emergency help takes over or the casualty breathes normally.

4 Press 30 times within 20 seconds, then give two rescue breaths. Perform another 30 compressions and two more rescue breaths. Continue like this until help arrives.

TOP TIP
If in doubt, dial 911. They will give you advice about what to do.

Stop severe blood loss

Severe bleeding can be potentially life threatening since it can cause shock and lead to unconsciousness. You will need to act very quickly to control it.

1 If possible, wash and dry your own hands. Then put on the disposable gloves in your first-aid kit to protect against infection.

2 Apply pressure to the wound with a pad or fingers to stem the bleeding. If a large object is embedded in the wound, leave it.

3 If a limb is injured, raise and support it. Treat for shock by laying the casualty down and keeping them warm.

4 If possible, apply a sterile dressing. Firmly bandage it, but not so tightly that it stops the circulation to fingers or toes.

5 If there is a large embedded object, cover it with a sterile dressing. Build up padding around the object, then bandage.

6 Call an ambulance. If blood seeps through, cover with a second bandage. If this fails, remove both and apply a new one.

Help a choking victim

An object lodged in the throat usually causes a fit of coughing. But it may block the throat so badly that the casualty cannot cough or even breathe.

1 If the casualty cannot cough up the object, give them up to five sharp blows between the shoulder blades, using the heel of your hand.

2 Check the mouth to see if the blows have dislodged the obstruction. If so, remove it. If not, go on to the next step.

3 From behind, place your fist between the belly button and rib cage, place your other hand on top and sharply pull in and up.

4 Give up to five of these abdominal thrusts. Check the mouth again to see if the obstruction has been dislodged.

5 If three cycles of blows and thrusts fail to remove the blockage, call an ambulance and keep trying to remove it.

Safety!
Due to their forceful nature, abdominal thrusts can injure the casualty, causing bruising and even broken ribs. Some authorities do not recommend them, but you may feel you have no choice.

Soothe a burn

The first priority with a burn is to cool the affected area and keep cooling it. This is because any heat in the injury can continue to cause burn damage. You must continue to cool the injury at least until it no longer hurts.

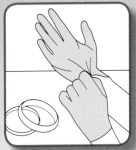

1 Hold the injury under cold, gently running water—or completely immerse it—for a minimum of ten minutes, and longer if it still hurts.

2 If possible, put on disposable gloves. Remove any watches, jewelry, or clothing from the injury unless they are stuck to the skin.

3 Cover the burn with clean, nonfluffy material such as a plastic bag or plastic wrap to protect it from infection.

4 If the burn is deep or larger than a postage stamp, it will need medical attention, so call an ambulance.

Pack a first-aid kit

If you are going anywhere out of range of swift medical care, you should pack a first-aid kit. You can buy one already prepared, but check that it includes these items:

- One package of disposable gloves
- Antiseptic wipes
- Ten sterile adhesive dressings
- Three medium sterile dressings
- One large sterile dressing
- One extra-large sterile dressing
- One large sterile bandage
- Microporous tape
- One triangular bandage
- One sterile eye pad
- Six safety pins
- Tweezers
- Scissors

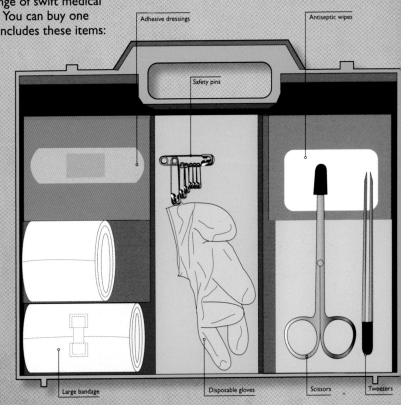

Adhesive dressings

Antiseptic wipes

Safety pins

Large bandage

Disposable gloves

Scissors

Tweezers

Wrap a sling

If someone injures his or her arm—possibly even breaking it—you can help relieve the pain by supporting and protecting it in a sling. Normally you should tie this so that the hand is slightly higher than the elbow, with the sling covering most of the hand.

1 Ask the victim to sit down and support her forearm on the injured side, with the wrist and hand slightly higher than the elbow. If she cannot support her own arm like this, provide support or get some help.

2 Slide one end of a triangular bandage between the elbow and chest so that the long side is upright near the hand, the opposite point is beyond the elbow, and the top point is wrapped around the neck.

3 Lift the lower part of the bandage up over the forearm and tie it to the part that is draped around the victim's neck. Tie a reef knot in the hollow above the collarbone (see page 148 for how to tie the knot).

4 Bring the point of the bandage near the elbow forward and secure it to the front of the sling with a safety pin, if available. If not, simply twist the fold at the point and tuck it between the bandage and the arm.

5 Check for restricted circulation by pressing one of the fingernails until it turns white, then releasing it. It should turn pink again, showing that the blood has flowed back. If it doesn't, adjust the sling until it does.

Fashion a splint

A fracture is a serious injury that requires expert medical help, but you may need to secure the broken limb in an emergency.

Lower arm
For a fracture of the lower arm or wrist, carefully place a folded newspaper, or heavy piece of clothing under the arm. Tie it in place with pieces of cloth or tape and put the arm in a sling.

Leg or ankle
A lower leg or ankle [fract]ure can be splinted in [the] same way as an arm, [w]rapping a newspaper [or b]ulky garment around [th]e limb and securing it.

Hip or pelvis
Ideally, anyone with a hip or pelvis fracture should not be moved. If this is not possible, strap the legs together with a towel in between and keep them still until the emergency services arrive.

Treat a cut

If a cut is not bleeding so dramatically that it needs special techniques to stop severe blood loss (see page 141), treat it as a minor wound.

1 Wash your own hands under hot water to kill or remove anything that might infect the wound. Dry them on a clean towel.

2 Cover any cuts on your own hands and put on disposable gloves from the first-aid kit to prevent cross infection.

3 If the cut is dirty, clean it under running water. Gently pat it dry with a sterile dressing or any clean lint-free material.

4 Cover the cut and use soap and water to clean the surrounding skin. Then carefully pat it dry.

5 Cover the cut with either an adhesive dressing or a larger sterile dressing held on with adhesive tape.

6 If possible, raise the affected area above the level of the heart.

Fishing line   Hooks

Short log

Bait (such as worms)

Hook a fish

You don't need a fishing rod to hook a fish—just hooks, line, and bait. If you want, you can make your own hooks from bent wire or pins or even sharp thorns. It's best to use three or four hooks at once, attached to a fixed line.

TOP TIP
If your catch is too small to eat, throw it back in the water. Otherwise, kill it quickly by hitting it on the head with something hard.

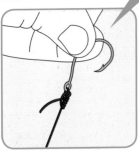

1 For each hook, cut a length of nylon line about 3 ft (90 cm) long. Tie a hook to each line using the clinch knot shown above, which will not slip.

2 Tie the other end of each line to a log, with one line at each end and the other lines in the middle. The hooks need to dangle below the log.

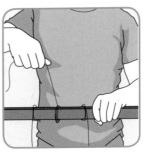

3 Tie a long length of line—at least 33 ft (10 m)—to the log. This acts as a large float. Thread some bait onto each hook, making sure it is secure.

4 Attach the main line to a small tree and toss the float into the water. Pull it in every half hour to see if you have caught anything, or if you see the float moving.

You will need:

Sticks

Sharp knife

A source of fresh, clean water and a campfire

Clean and cook a fish

Fish are best eaten fresh, so why not prepare the fish you've caught right there on the riverbank or beach and barbecue them over a campfire? They'll taste better than any fish you've ever eaten before.

Safety!
Cutting a fish open demands a very sharp knife, so ask an adult to help you with this.

1 Look for four sticks that are strong enough to support your fish skewer over a fire. You'll also need a thin stick to use as a skewer. When you find one, sharpen one end.

2 Take the fish to a place where you can clean it. Slit the belly open from the hole at the back (anus) to just behind the gills. Try not to push the knife in too far.

3 Pull the fish apart and use the knife to scrape out the internal organs. Dispose of them carefully, so you don't attract dangerous animals. Wash the fish.

4 Push the sharp end of the skewer stick through the mouth of the fish, along the backbone, and through the flesh of the tail. If the fish spins on one skewer, use two.

Troll for mackerel

If you are out in a small boat at sea, you can use a hand line to catch fast-swimming mackerel and other fish by trailing a lure (artificial bait) behind the moving boat. This is called trolling.

1 Tie a weight 10 ft (3 m) from the end of a fishing line. Using a clinch knot (see opposite page), attach a lure to the end of the line.

2 Throw the lure and weight over the side of the boat. Quickly let the line out to keep it away from the propeller.

3 Use one hand to hold the spool and the other to feel the tension on the line. If the lure rises to the surface, slow the boat down.

4 When a fish bites, you should feel more tension on the line. Reel in your catch, unhook it, and hit it on the head to kill it.

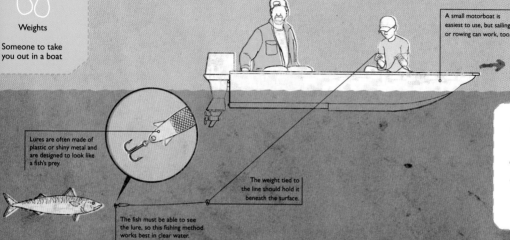

A small motorboat is easiest to use, but sailing or rowing can work, too.

Lures are often made of plastic or shiny metal and are designed to look like a fish's prey.

The weight tied to the line should hold it beneath the surface.

The fish must be able to see the lure, so this fishing method works best in clear water.

Important!
Never take a boat out on the sea without an adult who has experience of the local tides and currents.

Build a fish trap

In shallow streams, you can trap fish by building a rock wall across a shallow area where they feed at night. The wall stops them from escaping back into deep water.

5 Push the support sticks into the ground on both sides of the fire and wedge the skewer between them. Cook the fish until the flesh flakes when tested with a knife.

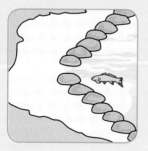

1 Build a wall of rocks across the edge of the shallow area, but leave a narrow V-shaped entrance where the current flows in. At night the fish will swim in to feed but will find it difficult to swim out again.

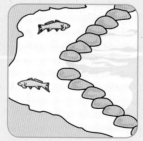

2 Check the trap in the early morning and scoop out any big fish with a net. Allow the other fish to escape by making a large gap in the rock wall. If you won't be using the trap again, take it apart.

Flick of the hand
It is possible to catch fish such as trout with your bare hands. If you know where a fish is hiding, lie belly down on the bank and slowly ease your hand under its belly. Move your hand toward its head and, smoothly but firmly, tighten your grip and toss it onto the bank.

Firewood

Lighter or matches

Water and water carrier

Light a campfire

A fire is a big morale booster when you are camping. It keeps you warm, gives you something to cook on, and is endlessly fascinating to watch. Starting and keeping a fire burning is not always easy, even if you have a lighter or matches. You need the right fuel and lots of it. You also need to take care not to start a wildfire, so don't be foolish out there.

TOP TIP

Build your fire near a stream or a pool so that you can use water to control or put it out.

Important!

Ask a responsible person to choose a good site for the fire, with no overhanging trees or bushes and clear of inflammable debris. A patch of bare earth is best.

1 Make a platform of small fuel wood, roughly 1 ft (30 cm) square, to keep the fire off the damp ground so that it burns more easily. If the ground is very damp, use two layers of wood.

2 Make a bundle of tinder roughly the size of two fists and put it in the middle of the fire platform. Make sure you have enough tinder for a second attempt if your first burns out.

3 Cover this with two or three handfuls of your smallest, driest kindling so that you can only just see the tinder—but leave a gap so that you can insert a match to light it.

4 Light the tinder with a match or a lighter. Using a lighter can be awkward, so it's easier to light a thin roll of paper first and then poke the burning end into the fire.

5 When the fire catches, put more small kindling over the flames. Add thicker kindling, then stack small fuel around the fire in a cone shape. When this is burning well, add thicker fuel.

Types of firewood

Tinder
You need this to start the fire. Dry paper is good. Otherwise try dead fern foliage, birch bark, dry creepers, dead leaves, or dead grass. It must be fine and papery and bone dry.

Kindling
To turn a small flame into a fire, you need slender, dry dead sticks ranging from the width of a match to pencil size. Avoid sticks that have been lying flat on the ground, they won't be dry enough.

Small fuel
At first you will need sticks about as thick as your thumb and around 1 ft (30 cm) long. Dry dead wood is best, as with kindling, but green wood such as birch will also burn if it is dry.

Logs
When the fire gets going, add thicker wood. Logs that are too thick to break over your knee are useful, as they keep your fire burning for several hours.

Put it out
Don't start a bush fire! Never leave a burning fire behind you. When it has died down, spread the embers so that they cool, then soak them with a lot of water until they are completely cold. Then scatter the wet embers.

Cook outdoors

Once you have a fire going, you can use it for cooking. Unless you are simply boiling water, it's no use trying to cook over a blaze. You must wait for the flames to die down to hot embers. You can always throw more fuel on the fire to build it up to a blaze again when you're finished cooking your meal.

Tripod
An easy, stable way of supporting a kettle or cooking pot over a fire is to use a tripod. It is best suited to heating water, soup, or food being cooked in liquid. Tie three green sticks together to make the tripod and use a fourth branched stick as a hook.

Soak the sticks in water, such as a nearby stream, for a while to make sure that they will not burn.

HOT ROCKS
An ancient method of cooking is to build a fire on a bed of flat stones, then brush away the embers and cook food on the hot stones.

You can rake the hot embers toward the back so that they give less heat at the front.

Grill
Once the fire has died down, you can surround it with stones and use these to support a metal grill. A shelf from an old domestic oven is ideal. Use this to heat metal pans and, when it gets very hot, to barbecue food on skewers.

Cooking in foil
You can wrap food in tinfoil to make a package that you cook directly in the embers. The foil keeps the food clean, helps stop it from burning, and seals in the juices. You can cook all types of things like this, from whole fish to vegetable stews.

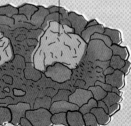

Use a double layer of foil for each package—one is not thick enough.

Use your fire-making skills to barbecue fish on page 144.

Tie useful knots

You never know when you'll need to tie a few knots. There are many types of knots, but most are needed only for specific tasks. If you learn the ones shown here, you'll be equipped for the vast majority of situations.

go to pages 144–145 to tie the fishing line and hook a fish.

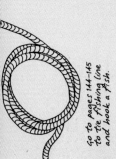

TOP TIP
Rope with a thickness of at least 0.5 in (1 cm) is best for practicing these knots.

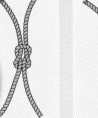

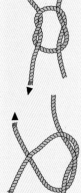

Reef knot

The trick with this knot is to make the two pieces of rope the same shape. This knot is commonly used to join two lines of equal size.

Double sheet bend

This knot is ideal for joining two lines together, especially lines of different thickness. If that is the case, use the thinner line to tie the knot.

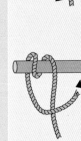

Clove hitch

Though not very sturdy, this knot can be used for tying a rope to a post. You can make the two loops first and drop them over the post afterward.

Round turn

This knot is formed by making a round turn and is secured by two loops. The round turn part on the post is what takes the strain.

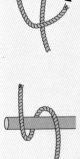

Fisherman's bend

Though difficult to untie if there is tension on the line, this knot is very secure. It is often used to attach anchors and valuable items of fishing equipment.

Bowline

The bowline is used to make a secure loop in the end of a line and can be used for a wide variety of jobs on land and on the water.

Make a lariat

The classic lariat is made of firm leather and often employs a metal ring instead of a knot, but you can make your own with a stiff length of rope and a honda knot.

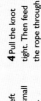

Tie a knot here to keep the lariat's shape.

Feed this end through the loop to finish.

1 Make a loose loop in the rope and slip the end through it.

2 Pull the end back up through the loop.

3 Tighten the left loop, leaving a small eye in the rope.

4 Pull the knot tight. Then feed the rope through.

Lasso a chair

Well over 100 years ago, Mexican cowhands used a noose called *la riata* to rope or lasso cattle. The cowboys of the American West learned the trick but shortened the name of the knot to *lariat*. If you don't have any cows nearby, try lassoing a chair!

You will need:

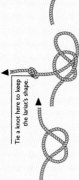

Rope

Chair

Cowboy hat

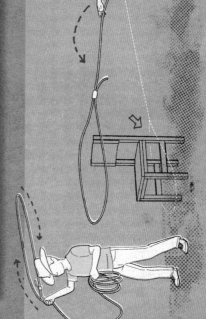

1 Take the coil in your left hand. Make a noose about 24 in (60 cm) across and hold it tightly in your right hand, above the knot.

2 Hold the lasso out to the side and begin to rotate it in a clockwise motion. Relax your wrist so that it moves fluidly.

3 Begin to swing the lasso noose over your head from right to left. Swing the rope as if it were a wheel revolving around your wrist.

4 Aim at your target as you extend your hand forward and bring it down to shoulder level. The noose should shoot forward.

5 If you get it right, the noose should encircle the target. Pull back on the rope to tighten the noose. Yee-haw! You've just lassoed your first chair!

149

Watch wildlife

Wild animals are very wary, and they see anything strange as a threat, including you! To stand any chance of getting close enough for a good view, you need to convince them that you are just part of the landscape. This means trying to be inconspicuous, moving as quietly as possible, and being very, very patient.

Binoculars

Binoculars transform wildlife watching. You can get different types, but 8x30 binoculars are a good choice. Avoid those with zoom lenses. Find out how to adjust them to suit your eyes and carry them around your neck on a short strap.

Disguise yourself with muted colors, but don't wear the same shade all over, as this makes your human shape obvious. Break it up with darker and paler clothing.

On sunny days, shade your eyes with a hat rather than sunglasses, which can alter your perception of color.

If you see an animal, keep watching it while bringing your binoculars up to your eyes. Don't lose sight of it!

When you get very good, the animals won't know you are watching them.

Use a backpack to carry food, water, field guides, a map, and spare clothes.

Take waterproof clothing if you think it might rain, but avoid materials such as nylon that rustle as you move.

If you start early (always a good idea), wear several layers to stay warm. Take them off as the temperature rises.

TOP TIP

Mask your scent. Don't use strong perfumes and avoid strongly flavored snacks.

Read tracks

You can improve your chances of seeing wild animals by learning a few basic tracking skills. Look for these signs, and if you watch and wait nearby, you may see the animals that left them.

Signs of trails
Look for flattened trails in the grass and places where animals regularly cross streams.

Animal hair
Tufts of animal hair are not difficult to identify, if you have some idea which animals live in the area.

Footprints
Check soft ground for footprints. You will probably have a good idea of what type of creature made them.

Stripped bark
Deer, rabbits, and hares all strip bark from trees. Big claw marks mean that there are bears around!

How to move

1 As you walk, carefully and slowly place each foot down. Try to avoid stepping on sticks that might snap, rustling against bushes, and dislodging rocks. Wild animals have acute hearing and are easily spooked by odd sounds.

2 If you see an animal, stop calmly, raise your binoculars swiftly but quietly, and stay still. If you don't move, you will be virtually invisible.

3 Listen. Can you hear birds moving through the trees toward you? Scan around without focusing too hard on one thing and you may see a flicker of movement. If you stay still, the birds may come and feed right in front of you.

4 Try to stay downwind of mammals, such as deer or foxes, so that the wind carries your scent away from them. If you are upwind, they will detect you and run off. This doesn't matter with birds, which have a poor sense of smell.

5 Above all, be patient. You may get to a good viewpoint and see nothing, but don't just move on. Watch and wait. Relax. Enjoy being part of the wildlife.

Hoot like an owl

You can make a very convincing owl hoot by blowing into your cupped hands. Try it. You might even get a reply!

1 Hold up your hands in front of your mouth and put the edge of your right hand against the heel of your left hand so that they form a rough L shape.

2 Fold your fingers inward so that your hands form a hollow ball, with the sides of your thumbs pressed together. Make sure there are no gaps.

3 Spread your thumbs to make a small gap. Press your lips against the gap and blow. You should be able to make a breathy, quavering owl hoot.

Squeak like a mouse

Use a variation of the owl-hoot technique to make a shrill squeal, like a mouse. You might even attract a fox!

1 Place a fresh green blade of grass between your thumbs and press them together. The grass blade must be stretched tight.

2 Flare the fingers of both hands, put your lips to the gap between your thumbs, and blow. The grass should vibrate to create a high-pitched squeak.

3 Try using thicker and thinner blades of grass. A thicker one will make a lower rasp, while a thinner one will make a high squeal. You can also blow in short bursts instead of one long note.

You can use this technique to chirp or warble like a small songbird.

Count birds

See that flock of birds flying your way? How many are there? How can you count them?

Discover how to attract birds to your home by learning how to feed them on pages 98–99.

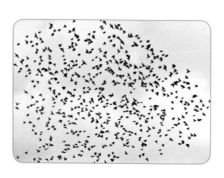

One block at a time

Look hard and count a "block" of, say, 100 by counting roughly ten across and ten down. Then judge how many of these blocks you could fit into the whole area covered by the airborne flock. In this image, there are roughly six of these blocks, which, multiplied by 100, gives 600 birds. Try it. If the flock is much smaller, try counting five times five instead, to give blocks of 25.

Owl pellets
This pellet of hair and bone may have been coughed up by an owl roosting in the branches above.

BE A SPORTS HERO

Time for fun and games, with bikes, boats, boards, and lots of balls to hit, kick, bowl, tap, strike, shoot, and slam-dunk. Pick up some tips and tricks for improving your techniques at familiar games and find out about some new sports. Plus, there are lots of ideas for crazy games to play with friends.

Juggle a soccer ball

A great way to improve your agility and control of a soccer ball is to practice keeping a ball in the air using your feet and knees. It takes a little bit of patience at first, but once you get started, it can be addictive! Why not compete against your friends to see who can keep the ball up in the air the longest?

1 Drop the ball and kick it back up to your hands with the top part of your dominant foot. Keep practicing until you can do it easily and then try it with your other foot.

2 Once you have mastered this, try kicking the ball with your foot to the top part of your knee and bouncing it there before you catch it.

3 As you progress, increase the number of times you kick or knee the ball up before you catch it. How many times can you bounce the ball without dropping it?

4 Next, try to switch the ball from foot to foot and knee it up a few times, too. Try to keep going without catching it or without the ball dropping to the ground.

5 Controlling the power and direction of your touches takes a little getting used to, but after awhile, you should be able to keep it in the air with ease.

World Cup

If you don't have enough players for a proper match, try this game, often called World Cup, for some fun. It works for four players or more. You need a volunteer to be goalkeeper and the rest of you can either play singly, or in teams of two or three.

1 In round one, the keeper throws out the ball and the players battle to score. When you, or your team score, you stand out. The last to score is eliminated.

2 Round two is the same, except that players have to score two goals.

3 In round three, you have to score three goals to stay in. Continue the rounds with three goals as the target (or it becomes boring for the spectators) until only one team is left the winner.

4 Change goalkeeper and start again.

> **TOP TIP**
> *Try heading the ball, too, or using other parts of your body to keep it up in the air, like your heels or shoulders!*

Learn the Raí flick

Getting around defenders can sometimes be tough, so how about going over their heads using this trick, named after the Brazilian midfielder?

1 Advance with the ball toward the defender. As you get close to your opponent, let the ball roll on a little bit and then hop on it so that your feet grip the ball on both sides.

Gripping the ball like this makes it harder for the defender to tackle you.

2 Jump again, this time lifting the ball with your feet behind you. Try to launch the ball over your shoulder and the defender by flicking it up with the back of your heel.

Dive for the ball

As the last line of defense, goalkeepers need lightning-quick reactions, catlike agility, and these basic techniques to become excellent shot stoppers.

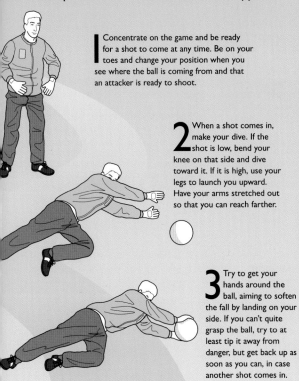

1 Concentrate on the game and be ready for a shot to come at any time. Be on your toes and change your position when you see where the ball is coming from and that an attacker is ready to shoot.

2 When a shot comes in, make your dive. If the shot is low, bend your knee on that side and dive toward it. If it is high, use your legs to launch you upward. Have your arms stretched out so that you can reach farther.

3 Try to get your hands around the ball, aiming to soften the fall by landing on your side. If you can't quite grasp the ball, try to at least tip it away from danger, but get back up as soon as you can, in case another shot comes in.

Score a penalty

It requires nerves of steel to take a good penalty shot, especially because everyone is watching you. Here's how the greats do it.

1 Practice taking penalties in an open net first and then with a goalkeeper. The areas in red in the picture above are the hardest areas for the goalkeeper to reach. See which angles suit your style best and work more on those.

2 When you're taking a penalty in a game, decide where you want to hit the kick and then stick to that plan. Try to give the goalkeeper no clues as to where you want to kick the ball—or bluff by looking where you don't intend on kicking it.

3 Remember your plan and make a short run up to the ball. Don't blast the ball when you kick it, as you'll have less control over the shot. If the goalkeeper saves, be ready for any possible rebounds— you can still score even if you miss the first shot!

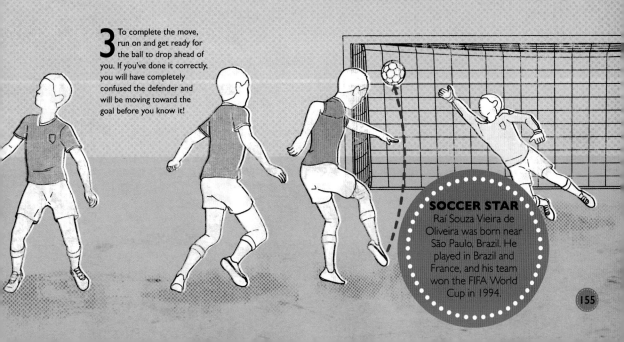

3 To complete the move, run on and get ready for the ball to drop ahead of you. If you've done it correctly, you will have completely confused the defender and will be moving toward the goal before you know it!

SOCCER STAR
Raí Souza Vieira de Oliveira was born near São Paulo, Brazil. He played in Brazil and France, and his team won the FIFA World Cup in 1994.

Bat better in cricket

The goal of cricket is to score as many runs as possible without being bowled out. A typical strategy is to bat defensively at first and then attack later. Here are the main shots you can use, but deciding which shot to use and when is up to you.

General stance
When awaiting the bowler's delivery, you should be "side on" to the bowler. Put your weight on the balls of your feet so that you can change your stance when the ball comes in.

Your feet should be about 1 ft (30 cm) apart.

Keep your elbow high so that your weight is behind the bat.

Backward defensive
To defend the wicket from a ball that is bouncing close to you, pull the bat up into a vertical column. The ball should drop harmlessly in front of you after it hits the bat.

Create a solid defense by holding the bat close to your leg pad.

Forward defensive
By taking a step forward, you can snuff out a ball that is close to you so that it doesn't bounce high. The trick here is to keep your eyes on the ball and position the bat so that the ball hits its middle.

Cover drive
Use this shot if you want to attack a ball that is a little out of your reach. As the ball hurtles down the field, step forward and keep your bat straight.

Firmly strike the ball along the ground.

Square cut
When the bowler delivers the ball wide and short, it's time to bring a big-hitting swing out! Watch the ball closely, however, as the bowler might have spun it so that it bounces back in toward your body or the wicket.

Take a small step backward to give you room to swing.

Play cricket anywhere

No matter where you are, whether it's a garden, backyard, or a beach, you can put your batting and bowling skills into practice for an informal game of cricket. All you need is a cricket bat and a tennis ball, and a wicket of some description. Any number of players can play, and all you have to decide is who does what and which rules to use.

The wicket can be anything—some wood or sticks, a tree, a cardboard box, or body board in the sand. Put a marker on the other side to run to.

Choose the rules
Once you've set up your game and picked who is going to bat, it's time to decide what the rules are. Here are some of the most common ones players use:

• You might just want to play for fun, so decide if you want to count the runs or not at the start.
• You can't be called out on your first ball, or if you haven't scored.
• Six is the maximum score per strike.
• If you hit the ball you've got to run.
• The player who gets the batter out bats next.
• If the batter hits the ball out of the playing area, he scores a six and is out.

itch in baseball

To pitch well in baseball, there are two things you need to master. The first is how you hold the ball (see right), as varying grips and wrist movements make the ball move in different ways. The second is the pitching motion (below), which should be smooth, balanced, and consistent.

Wind-up
Set the ball in your hand with your chosen grip. Then, standing with one foot on the pitching rubber, raise one leg (the one opposite your throwing hand) straight up. Don't lean too far backward or forward.

Stride
Without pausing, step forward towards home plate with your raised leg, and reach back with your pitching hand. Turn your chest, shoulders, and hips quickly toward home as you pull your arm forward to release the ball.

Pitch
As you land your weight on your front foot, release the ball toward the plate, keeping your eyes on the target. Follow through so that you move into a safe fielding position. The ball might be coming right back at you!

Great grips
Being able to mix up your grips and throws is the best way to fool the batter. Here are some of the most common grips.

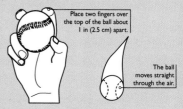

Place two fingers over the top of the ball about 1 in (2.5 cm) apart.

The ball moves straight through the air.

Four-seam fastball
The four-seam fastball is the most common and fastest pitch in baseball. Don't grip the ball too tightly, and make sure there is a gap between the ball and your palm.

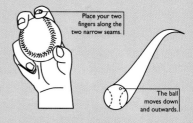

Place your two fingers along the two narrow seams.

The ball moves down and outwards.

Two-seam fastball
Gripped tighter than the four-seam fastball, the two-seam version is a little bit slower. It is sometimes called a "sinker" as it drops low as it approaches the batter.

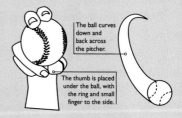

The ball curves down and back across the pitcher.

The thumb is placed under the ball, with the ring and small finger to the side.

Slider
The third-fastest pitch in baseball after the two fastballs, the slider differs because it curves. Batters often think it's just a normal fastball and won't be ready for this.

TOP TIP
Professional pitchers and catchers use hand signals to communicate to each other before a pitch—try to develop some signals with your friends.

Serve in tennis

The ability to hit a powerful serve is a great weapon to have in tennis. In fact, some players base their entire strategy on their service game, hoping to prevent their opponents from returning the ball. Here's how they do it.

Try to hit the ball with the center of the racket.

Keep your eye on the ball at all times.

Your shoulder and arm should feel slightly stretched.

I Throw the ball high up in front of you with your left hand and bend your left knee forward, moving hand and knee together.

Driving your feet and legs up and forwards enables you to hit the ball harder.

Bend your knees as you hit the ball so that all of your energy is transferred to the racket.

2 Turn your body slightly away from the court and move your racket hand back behind you, ready to strike the ball as it reaches the top of the throw.

3 Swing your racket up, hitting the ball as hard as you can and in the direction of the corner.

Bounce along in ping-pong

Ping pong, or table tennis, is exciting, fast-moving, and very physical. By simply bouncing the ball on your paddle, you can improve your coordination and control of the ball.

I First see how long you can keep the ball bouncing on your paddle.

2 When you master this, try alternating the sides of the paddle for each bounce.

3 For extra difficulty, see if you can do this as you walk or run—or with a paddle in both hands and bouncing the ball between them.

Get to grips

Of the many ways to hold the paddle, the two below are the most common.

Shakehand grip

(front)   (back)

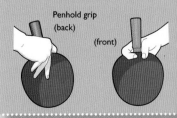

The shakehand grip (above) is perhaps the most popular, but the penhold grip (below) is favored by Chinese players in particular.

Penhold grip

(back)

(front)

Sneak a hot dog

The "hot dog"—or the between-the-legs shot—can be played if you are chasing the ball and don't have the time to turn around and return it back over the net.

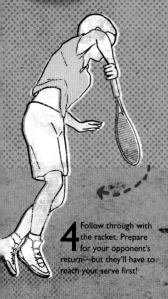

Raise your racket so it is at a 90-degree angle to your chest

4 Follow through with the racket. Prepare for your opponent's return—but they'll have to reach your serve first!

1 Start with your feet wide apart, back to the net, and a tennis ball in hand. Drop the ball, letting it bounce once. Get ready to hit it with your racket as it comes up.

2 When the ball bounces up to about shin level, hit it between your legs. Try to hit it up but not too high or it will hit you. Once you've got the hang of it, try doing it as you run.

Hit a drop shot in badminton

Hitting the shuttlecock so that it drops just over the net is an essential part of badminton. Mastering killer drop shots will send your opponent dashing all over the court in order to return them.

1 Face the net, lean on your back foot, and prepare your wrist and elbow for the swing.

2 The way you angle your racket determines where the shot goes (see left). Decide which shot to play.

3 Hit the shuttlecock high in front of you, stepping forward and straightening your elbow as you strike it.

4 Develop backhand skills by trying to hit the shot with your shoulder or back facing the net.

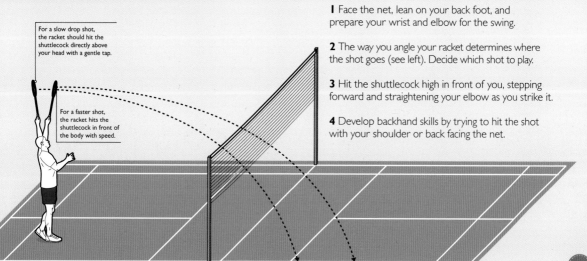

For a slow drop shot, the racket should hit the shuttlecock directly above your head with a gentle tap.

For a faster shot, the racket hits the shuttlecock in front of the body with speed.

Nail a free throw

In basketball, a free throw may be worth only one point, but this can be the difference between winning and losing. Here are some tips to improve your technique.

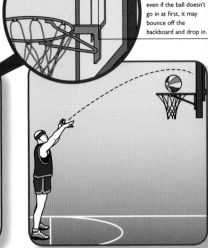

Aim for the backboard—even if the ball doesn't go in at first, it may bounce off the backboard and drop in.

1 Stand just behind the free-throw line and wait for the referee to signal that you can take the throw.

2 Cradle the ball in your weaker hand and have your stronger hand ready behind it, which will provide the thrust of the throw.

3 Slightly bend your knees and release the ball with your fingertips. Ideally, the ball should travel in an arc and sink into the net.

Learn basketball moves

As basketball is a noncontact sport, you have more time with the ball to develop your skills. Using these tips, you can practice some ice-cool moves and be ready the next time you hit the court.

NBA GIANT
Standing 7 ft 7 in (2.31 m) tall, Manute Bol is the tallest player ever to play in the National Basketball Association (NBA) in the U.S.

Blind pass

If done successfully, the blind pass will fool even the best defense! The goal is to make your opponent think you will play the ball one way, but instead you pass it to a teammate to the other side of you, without looking at them.

Bounce pass

If an opponent is blocking you and you can't pass in the air or above them, try a bounce pass along the court. Pick a teammate for the pass and aim low so that the ball bounces up into their hands.

Your teammate must be ready for the pass—there is a chance your surprise pass will fool them, too!

Aim to one side of your opponent and away from their arms.

Spin the ball

Of no practical use on a basketball court but a lot fun nonetheless, here's a very simple trick that never fails to impress.

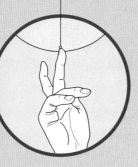

For extra control, try to balance the ball on your fingertips or fingernail, if it is not too long.

I The trick's hardest part is getting the start right. Using one hand, spin the ball in your hand and quickly transfer it to your fingers. Aim to have one finger in the center of the ball. It will take a few tries to get the balance right.

2 Keep your finger flexible so that it can adapt to how the ball moves. To keep it going, you can spin the ball with your free hand to gain more speed. Once you are good at this, try moving the ball to other fingers or from hand to hand.

Launch a tennis ball

For a fun trick, try placing a tennis ball on top of a basketball and letting both drop to the ground. As they bounce, the basketball will stop dead, but its energy will transfer to the tennis ball, launching it skyward!

Place the tennis ball on top of the basketball and drop both balls at the same time.

The tennis ball bounces off the basketball.

Bounce back to pages 10–11 to learn how to juggle.

Dribble skills

Have you ever seen players on TV transfer the ball to their other hand by bouncing it through their legs? As well as looking cool, it can be used to quickly change direction as you go on the offense.

Your hand should be ready for the ball as it bounces back up on the other side.

Have your feet about 18 in (45 cm) apart and bounce the ball at a spot between them.

Alley-oop!

The alley-oop is a complex but spectacular shot requiring two players. The first player throws the ball high up near the basket, and the other player jumps up, catches the ball, and directs it into the basket in one fluid movement. It may be difficult to execute, but it is beautiful to watch.

The passer must throw close to both the basket and their teammate.

The slam dunk

The last part of the alley-oop is a slam dunk, but this can also be performed with only one player running up and slamming the ball into the basket. A slam dunk not only gains two points for the team, but it also makes the crowd go wild.

You need to jump as high as you can while still controlling the ball in order to perform a great slam dunk.

Dodge the ball

If you want to play a game that doesn't take itself too seriously, dodge ball is the one for you! In dodge ball, your goal is to knock all your opponents out of the game by hitting them with soft foam balls. The official rules state that there are between six and ten players on a team (with a maximum of four substitutes), but to set up a game with your friends, any number can play.

1 The game can be played almost anywhere. All you need is a rectangular space, divided into three. The two teams each take one third of the court, at either end, and the referee places six balls in the strip between them, called the dead zone. No balls may be thrown in this zone.

2 When the whistle is blown, players run to get the balls and bring them back to their third of the court, where they can throw them. When throwing, aim below the shoulders, and the ball must not bounce before hitting your target.

3 If a thrown ball hits an opposition team member, that player is out and must sit at the side until allowed back on. If a thrown ball is caught by the opposition team, they can bring one of their players back on, and the throwing player is out.

4 You can pass the ball a maximum of three times to your teammates, but the ball must be thrown within five seconds. The length of a dodgeball match should be decided in advance. If the time elapses, the team with the most players is declared the winner. Happy dodging!

TOP TIP
Substitutes can be brought on if a player gets injured or if either team uses its one time-out.

Bowl a strike

Don't worry if you're throwing gutter balls every time—all is not lost. Put these tips into practice and you'll soon be hitting a strike!

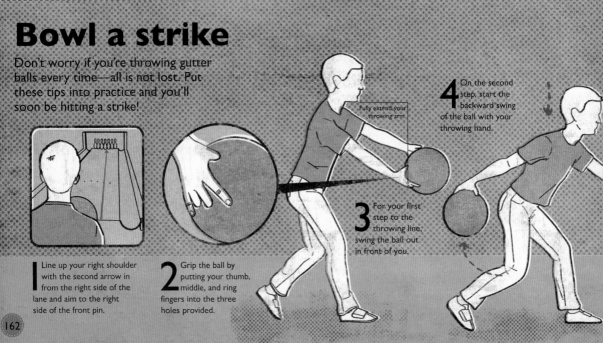

Fully extend your throwing arm.

4 On the second step, start the backward swing of the ball with your throwing hand.

3 For your first step to the throwing line, swing the ball out in front of you.

1 Line up your right shoulder with the second arrow in from the right side of the lane and aim to the right side of the front pin.

2 Grip the ball by putting your thumb, middle, and ring fingers into the three holes provided.

Control your cue

There's more to pool than just hitting balls into pockets—by playing these shots below, you can change the way your cue ball moves after the shot, making it easier for your next shot.

Making a bridge

Your weaker hand forms a bridge to enable the shot to be taken. The cue is placed in the V shape made between your thumb and index finger.

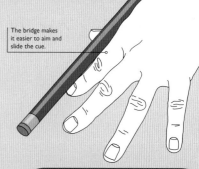

The bridge makes it easier to aim and slide the cue.

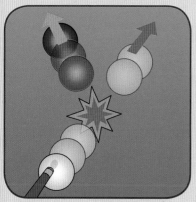

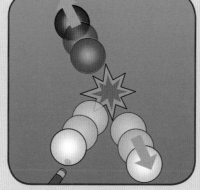

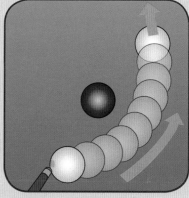

Topspin

If you want the cue ball to roll forward after making contact with another ball, try hitting the cue ball above the center (marked by the black dot, right).

Center of ball

Backspin

Sometimes you need the ball to roll backward. To achieve this, you need to hit the cue ball below the center. Don't hit too low or the ball will jump.

Swerve

To make the ball bend around, you must hit it above the center, either to the left or right. If you hit it top left, it will eventually loop to the left, and vice versa on the right.

5 Swing the ball back high and slightly bend your knees as you get to the line.

The higher you swing back, the more powerful your shot will be.

PERFECT GAME
If a player scores a strike with every throw, they will get a score of 300, also known as a "perfect game."

6 In a fluid motion, bring the ball forward and release. After you release, your throwing hand should end up over your head. If you've got it right, a strike should be on the cards!

Throw a disk

The first recognizable flying plastic disks were invented by American Walter Frederick Morrison in the 1950s. They soon became a worldwide phenomenon, and these days they regularly outsell other sports items. Here are some tips on how to throw and catch them that will really have you in a spin.

Flying a forehand
Also known as a "flick" or "sidearm," the forehand is one of the three basic throws.

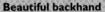

Let the disk droop down a little bit.

Make sure your thumb is on the outside of the disk, and that your index and middle fingers are on the inside.

Beautiful backhand
Here's the best way to give your backhand some style and power.

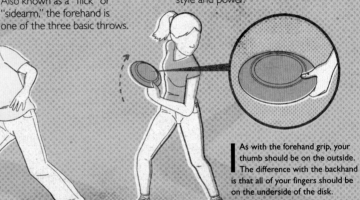

As with the forehand grip, your thumb should be on the outside. The difference with the backhand is that all of your fingers should be on the underside of the disk.

Keep your nonthrowing arm relaxed.

OUCH!
Before the use of plastic for flying disks, people threw around metal pie trays, which didn't glide as far as plastic and often injured players.

2 Sweep your throwing arm across the front of your body as you stand sideways and aim for your friend.

2 Build up power for your throw by moving the throwing side of your body back a little bit before you release the disk.

3 Throw the disk with a quick snap of your wrist.

3 Take a step forward with your leading foot as you release the disk. Once again, the trick is to get your wrist motion right.

Hammer time
The hammer throw is a lot like the forehand, but the disk is thrown vertically upward, not horizontally. Using the forearm grip, raise the disk above your head. Tilt your wrist down a little and then snap it forwards and upward as you release.

Play Ultimate

Once you've mastered the basic throws, why not set up a game of Ultimate, the most popular flying disk game? Light on rules but heavy on fun, Ultimate is extremely easy to play. The basic goal of the game is to score points by catching the disk in your opponents' end zone, with the winner being the first team to reach 17 goals.

TOP TIP
Colored shirts will help you figure out who is on your team.

59 ft (18 m)

END ZONE

END ZONE

120 ft (37 m)

end line

330 ft (100 m)

goal line

The playing field

These are the markings for the official version of the game, but all you really need is a strip of grass or concrete, with two end zones marked out, that both teams agree to play on. When a player throws the disk outside the area, play is restarted by the other team throwing it back in from the side.

How to play

1 Divide into two teams, with no more than seven players on each. Flip the disk to see who starts first. The attacking team starts from their opponents' end zone.

2 You can throw in any direction, but you're not allowed to run when you have the disk and can hold onto it for only ten seconds at a time.

3 This is a noncontact sport, so the defending team can only aim to intercept the disc in the air.

4 There is no referee in Ultimate, but players are expected to play fairly and treat one another with respect.

Try a cool catch

There are any number of ways you can catch the disk, ranging from simple two-handed takes to spectacular acrobatic twists and dives. Here are a few of the most common catches, but why not come up with some of your own?

Freestyling

These catches can be used to play Ultimate, but they have also taken on a life of their own in freestyle competitions. In these events, teams aim to come up with impressive combinations of moves and catches and earn points from judges based on difficulty, execution, and artistic impression.

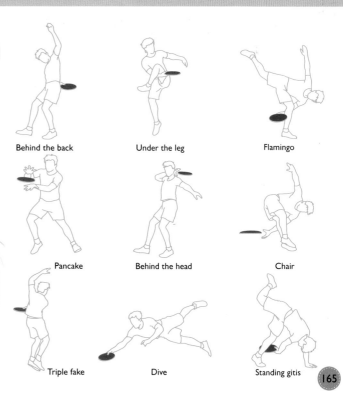

Behind the back

Under the leg

Flamingo

Pancake

Behind the head

Chair

Triple fake

Dive

Standing gitis

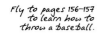
Fly to pages 156–157 to learn how to throw a baseball.

Perfect skateboard moves

Think you're a super skateboarder, amazing your friends with gravity-defying stunts? If you can roll on your board with confidence, it's time to try the tricks that you need to master if you want to wow the crowd at the skate park.

Ollie

1 This jump is crucial to almost all street-skating tricks. Try it first while stationary. Put your front foot just behind the front truck wheels, pointing slightly forward, and place the ball of your back foot on the tail behind the rear truck wheels, pointing slightly backward.

Back truck

Front truck

2 Crouch and push down hard with your back foot while taking all of the weight off your front foot. The front of the board will pop up. As the front rises, drag your front foot forward and lift your back foot.

3 As you lift your back foot, the board will take off. Control the front end with your front foot so that it levels out in midair.

Don't land with your weight on the middle of the deck

4 Land with your feet planted firmly over the trucks and with your knees bent to absorb the shock. Get this wrong and you'll snap your board. Now try it on the move.

TOP TIP
Don't skate in the rain—it won't work. You'll also soak your deck and get water in the wheel bearings, which will make them rusty.

Kickflip

1 This is like an ollie but with added flash, because you spin the board in midair. Start off in the same way, but with your front foot closer to the heel edge of the deck.

2 As you use your back foot to pop up the front of the board, flick the heel edge of the deck with the toes of your front foot in order to flip it. Lift your back foot clear to let it spin.

3 The board should flip right over and back upright. Keep your eye on the board and catch it at the right moment by planting your back foot on the deck first, then your front foot.

4 Land with your feet above the trucks and your knees bent to absorb the shock and then roll away. Try it again. Practice makes perfect.

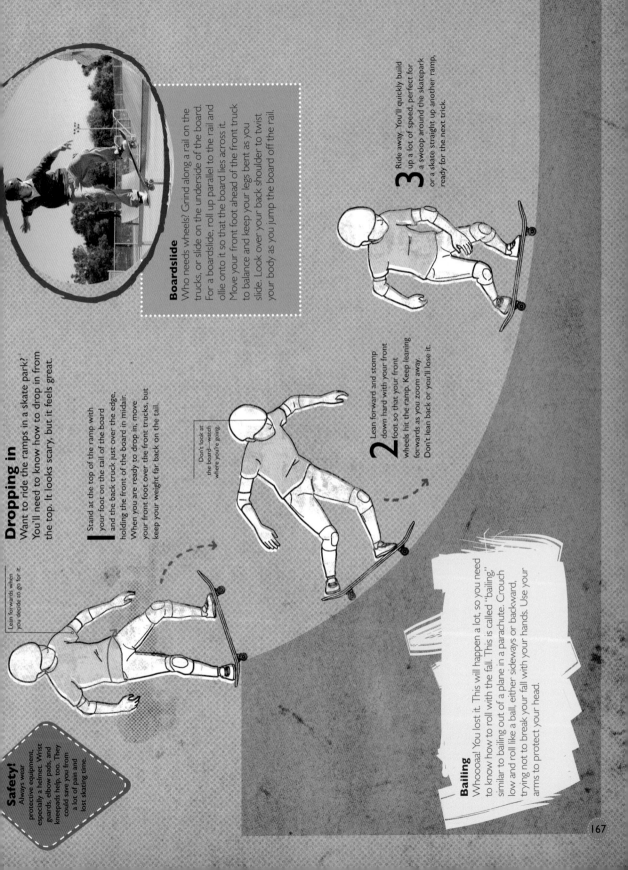

Dropping in

Want to ride the ramps in a skate park? You'll need to know how to drop in from the top. It looks scary, but it feels great.

> Lean forwards when you decide to go for it.

1 Stand at the top of the ramp with your foot on the tail of the board and the back truck just over the edge, holding the front of the board in midair. When you are ready to drop in, move your front foot over the front trucks, but keep your weight far back on the tail.

> Don't look at the board—watch where you're going.

2 Lean forward and stomp down hard with your front foot so that your front wheels hit the ramp. Keep leaning forwards as you zoom away. Don't lean back or you'll lose it.

Boardslide

Who needs wheels? Grind along a rail on the trucks, or slide on the underside of the board. For a boardslide, roll up parallel to the rail and ollie onto it so that the board lies across it. Move your front foot ahead of the front truck to balance and keep your legs bent as you slide. Look over your back shoulder to twist your body as you jump the board off the rail.

3 Ride away. You'll quickly build up a lot of speed, perfect for a swoop around the skatepark or a skate straight up another ramp, ready for the next trick.

Bailing

Whoooaa! You lost it. This will happen a lot, so you need to know how to roll with the fall. This is called "bailing," similar to bailing out of a plane in a parachute. Crouch low and roll like a ball, either sideways or backward, trying not to break your fall with your hands. Use your arms to protect your head.

167

Pull off some BMX tricks

You can have some serious fun on a BMX bike without leaving your backyard. Get started by learning a few basic tricks. Once you've got these down, you can start combining them into more complex, eye-popping stunts.

The pegs are where the front and back wheels join the frame of the bike.

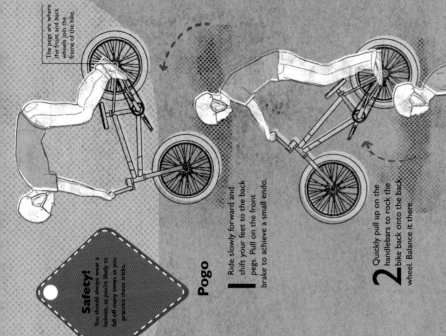

Pogo

| Ride slowly forward and shift your feet to the back pegs. Pull on the front brake to achieve a small endo.

2 Quickly pull up on the handlebars to rock the bike back onto the back wheel. Balance it there.

3 Once the bike is up and balanced, jump on the pegs to start hopping around on the back tire.

Wheelie

| Start pedaling before shifting your weight to the back of the bike. Pull up on the handlebars to lift the front wheel.

2 Find your balance point and keep pedaling. When you want to come down again, just shift your weight forward.

Endo

| Roll forwards and then squeeze the front brake as you shift your weight to the front of the bike.

2 As the back wheel comes off the ground, lean your body back a little to balance on the front wheel.

Bunnyhop

1 Roll slowly forwards with your toes turned down on the pedals. Get ready to pull up on the bars.

2 Pull the handlebars up to briefly lift the front wheel. As it goes down, kick the back of the bike up.

3 The whole bike should briefly be airborne, allowing you to jump up onto a ledge or over an obstacle.

4 Land on the back wheel first, or both wheels—never just the front wheel. Bend your arms and knees a little to absorb the shock.

TOP TIP
You can use a tire lever to get the tube back on the rim—but be careful not to trap or damage the tube.

Fix a flat tire

If you get a flat tire while out in the wilds, you can fix it with just a few simple tools. It may take a little time, but it's probably quicker than walking home pushing a bike with a flat tire! If you want, you can replace the inner tube with a brand-new one instead of repairing it, but you'll still need to know how to get it out of the tire.

You will need:

Tire repair kit or new inner tube

Set of three bike tire levers

Pump

1 Remove the wheel. Slip two tire levers between the rim and the tire and prize the tire over the rim. Hook the levers to the spokes.

2 Repeat with the third tire lever. Keep going until one side of the tire is off. Push the valve in and pull out the inner tube.

3 Pump up the inner tube and either feel for air coming from the hole or hold it underwater and watch for bubbles.

4 Use the sandpaper in the repair kit to scour the area around the hole. Apply a thin coat of rubber solution. Let it dry for five minutes.

5 Peel the backing off the patch and stick it over the hole. Press down hard for a minute. Ensure that the edges make good contact.

6 Lightly pump up the inner tube before putting it back, starting at the valve hole. Push the tire back onto the rim. It's hard work!

7 Push the valve in from the rim to check that the tube isn't trapped, then replace the wheel and pump up the tire. Fixed!

Snowboard a halfpipe

A halfpipe is essentially a large U-shaped bowl where snowboarders perform tricks. The tricks aren't suitable for beginners, though, so you will need to be a competent boarder before you try one.

The edge of the halfpipe is called the lip.

1 Drop in from the entry ramp at the top of the halfpipe and ride across the flat section up one of the walls toward the "lip."

2 Keep your board straight and try to build up speed so that you get enough "air," or height, from your jump.

3 When in the air, grab your board and spin your body in the direction of the turn. This trick is called an alley-oop.

TOP TIP

If there are other boarders on the halfpipe, use the time spent waiting to plan your run.

Ski jump

Olympic ski jumpers are capable of soaring to distances of more than 650 ft (250 m). If you have nerves of steel and think that you're a good skier, this is how it's done.

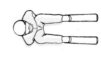

1 Begin your descent toward the ramp. Crouch down to minimize air resistance, keeping your legs parallel and your arms at your sides.

2 When you reach the section of the run where it begins to curve back upward, raise your hips and glide up the ramp, in preparation for the jump.

3 As you shoot off the ramp, leap both forward and upward at the same time. As you glide through the air, lean forward and make a large V shape with your skis to increase the surface area, which provides more lift.

4 As you come in to land, ensure that your skis are parallel and your body is in a squatting position. Slowly rise up and turn your skis to one side to slow down and come to a stop.

4 When you have completed your turn, release your grab on the board before you reach the lip on your way down.

5 Ride back across the bottom toward the other side. Learn some more tricks and get creative.

Snowboard tricks

Backside 720
Like an alley-oop, only much more difficult. The backside 720 requires you to make two full spins in the air. You need to get a lot of air if you want to pull off this trick.

Grind
Sliding your board across a surface is called grinding. Although it is typically performed on ramps or rails, you can also grind on the lip of a halfpipe.

McTwist
A McTwist is when you combine one and a half horizontal spins with a front vertical flip. Only the best snowboarders can master this trick.

Climb using ropes

Do you have a head for heights? Try these rock-climbing moves, but don't attempt them without the proper equipment, safety ropes, and an experienced climbing buddy who knows all of the tricks.

Foot and handholds

Learn these basic foot and handholds and how to plan a route. Test each hold for rock stability before trusting it with your weight.

Protrusions Use the entire sole of your boot.

Jugs These pockets make the safest holds.

Crevices Push your toe in, but don't wedge it.

Side pulls These help keep your balance.

Edges Use the inside edge of your boot on very small footholds.

Hand jams Push your thumb into your palm and arch your hand.

Belaying

Climbers work in pairs to scale rock faces using a system called belaying. The rope is anchored to the rock using steel rock screws and pins. As one partner climbs, the belayer feeds the rope through a device that locks onto the rope if it is pulled tight by a fall.

When the lead climber reaches a suitable spot, he will secure himself and act as the belayer.

Secure anchors are vital and are often left in place on popular rock faces.

The rope is attached to the rock at regular intervals.

The belayer feeds out the rope, keeping it as short as possible.

Safety!
Never climb alone, especially when you are starting out. You need someone to show you the ropes and how to use them to stop you from falling if you make a mistake.

Perfect a break roll

A break roll is a martial arts move that's very simple and useful in many situations. It is ideal for absorbing the impact of a jump onto a hard surface without risking injury.

1 Throw yourself forward, curving one arm down in front of your body.

Roll like a ball by holding your arm and shoulder in a smooth curve.

2 Topple onto your curved arm while pushing down with your other fist.

3 Roll over onto your shoulder, keeping your head clear of the ground.

Chimneying

If there is a tight gap between two rock faces with few handholds or footholds, you may be able to climb using the chimney technique.

1 Wedge yourself in the gap by bracing your back against the rear wall, but make sure you can freely move both your arms and legs.

2 Use your arms to push your back up the rock, and your legs can follow by walking up in small steps. Repeat this until you get to the top.

3 Once you are at the top, it may be difficult to get out of the chimney, so make sure that you have planned a way of getting over the ledge.

Rappel down again

Getting down a rock face is a lot quicker than climbing up it—if you have enough rope. You make a controlled descent "walking" backward down the rock face. This is called rapelling.

Low-stretch climbing ropes are securely anchored at the top of the rock face.

The descent is controlled by the rope running through the friction device.

A helmet is essential to protect you from falling debris.

The climber eases out the rope as she walks backward.

Safety!
Rappelling is a technique that you must be taught by a professional with all of the right equipment.

If you get it right, you can roll on concrete without hurting yourself.

Knowing how to safely roll out of trouble is a lifesaving skill.

RUN FREE
The break roll is one of the most important techniques of free running, which involves moving fast over obstacles such as walls and ledges.

4 Keep rolling smoothly like a ball so that you don't lose any of your momentum.

5 Bring your legs down so that your momentum throws you back on your feet.

6 Spring back upright. If you were moving fast, use the energy to keep moving.

Climb Mount Everest

Everest is the highest peak of the Himalayas, the loftiest mountain range on Earth. Despite this, it is not the hardest mountain to climb, provided you follow the standard route up the southeast ridge. The real dangers are the freezing conditions, howling winds, and extreme altitude, which can make breathing difficult and cause serious altitude sickness. If you want to get to the top of Everest, you need to be very fit, extremely determined, and you must carefully plan your expedition.

The summit

Camp IV
(High Camp)

Camp III

Camp II (ABC)

Camp I

Ridge route
The main route to the top is the southeast ridge, used by New Zealander Edmund Hillary and Sherpa Tenzing Norgay for the first ascent in 1953. The mountain can be climbed only in May, in the brief gap between winter and the summer monsoon.

Bad weather is the biggest problem for climbers and often forces them to turn back.

1 First, you must hike from Kathmandu in Nepal to Base Camp on the Khumbu Glacier. The hike takes 6–8 days, but helps you get used to the altitude of 17,700 ft (5,380 m). Most of your equipment is carried by local porters and pack animals.

2 From Base Camp you cross the Khumbu Icefall to reach Camp I at 19,900 ft (6,065 m). The icefall is a mass of tumbled ice with deep crevasses. Start well before dawn, when the freezing temperatures weld the ice blocks together.

3 Next you walk up the glacier of the Western Cwm. The deep ice is gashed by huge crevasses that bar the direct route to the upper valley and the base of the Lhotse face at 21,300 ft (6,500 m). This is the site of Camp II, or Advanced Base Camp (ABC).

From the summit you can see for more than 100 miles (160 km) and even make out the curvature of the Earth's surface.

Death zone

Conditions above 26,000 ft (8,000 m)—the stretch from Camp IV to the summit—are so extreme that the area is known as the "death zone." It is shockingly cold, and there is only half the normal level of oxygen. More than 200 climbers have died there, and most of the victims' bodies have never been recovered. Even highly experienced climbers find the death zone a struggle.

CHILL FACTOR

As you climb higher, the air gets colder. Mount Everest is the highest mountain on Earth, so not surprisingly it is also one of the coldest. Temperatures can drop as low as −76°F (−60°C), which is a lot colder than the North Pole!

4 Leaving Camp II, your next challenge is to ascend the icy Lhotse face, climbing with the help of fixed ropes left permanently in place. This takes you up to Camp III, which is located on a small ledge at 24,500 ft (7,470 m).

5 The route from Camp III is barred by the Geneva Spur—a big black rib of rock— and a region of hard yellow rock known as the Yellow Band. Fixed ropes help you pass these to reach Camp IV (High Camp) on the South Col at 26,000 ft (7,920 m).

6 From Camp IV you climb to the top. After a series of rock steps to reach the south summit, you continue along a knife-edged ridge to a 40-ft (12-m) rock wall called the Hillary Step. Finally, you climb a snow slope to the summit at 29,029 ft (8,848 m). You've made it!

Row a boat

You can take a small boat almost anywhere on a lake or slow-flowing river using a pair of oars and your own strength. It's easy, quiet, and satisfying and gives you a great feeling of harmony with the natural world. Rowing is also one of the best forms of exercise, especially if you do it competitively.

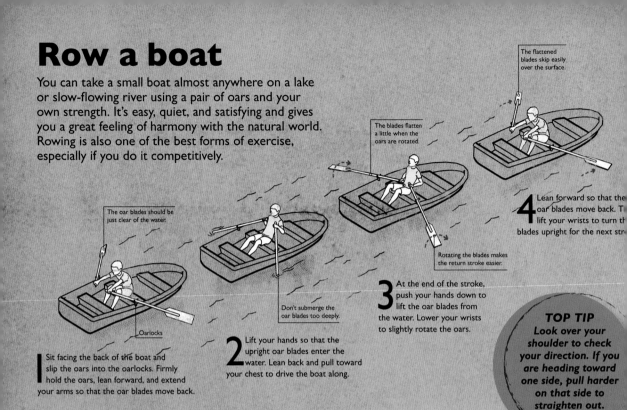

The flattened blades skip easily over the surface.

The blades flatten a little when the oars are rotated.

The oar blades should be just clear of the water.

Don't submerge the oar blades too deeply.

Rotating the blades makes the return stroke easier.

Oarlocks

1 Sit facing the back of the boat and slip the oars into the oarlocks. Firmly hold the oars, lean forward, and extend your arms so that the oar blades move back.

2 Lift your hands so that the upright oar blades enter the water. Lean back and pull toward your chest to drive the boat along.

3 At the end of the stroke, push your hands down to lift the oar blades from the water. Lower your wrists to slightly rotate the oars.

4 Lean forward so that the oar blades move back. T[hen] lift your wrists to turn th[e] blades upright for the next str[oke]

TOP TIP
Look over your shoulder to check your direction. If you are heading toward one side, pull harder on that side to straighten out.

Paddle a kayak

A kayak is a small canoe propelled by a two-bladed paddle, originally used by Arctic hunters. The cockpit may be completely open, or covered with a flexible spray skirt to keep the water out, but the basic paddling technique is similar.

1 Sit upright in the kayak with the balls of your feet against the foot supports. Hold the paddle with the smooth, hollow sides of the blades facing you.

2 Firmly grasp the paddle with your right hand and loosely with your left (or vice versa if left handed). Your hands should be a little more than shoulder width apart.

3 Swivel your body and extend your right arm as you pull your left arm back to take the first stroke. Dip the right paddle blade in the water and swivel back again, pulling back on the right side.

4 Bend the wrist of your tight-grip hand so that the paddle rotates in the other hand. This sets up the paddle blade to cleanly enter the water.

5 Dip the left paddle blade and swivel to pull it back. It won't be long before you stop thinking about how to do all of this and start enjoying yourself!

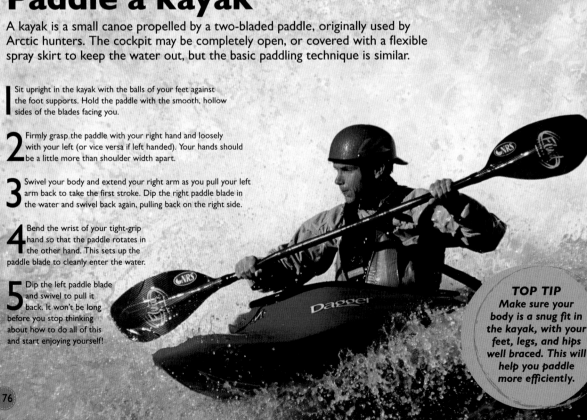

TOP TIP
Make sure your body is a snug fit in the kayak, with your feet, legs, and hips well braced. This will help you paddle more efficiently.

Sail a dinghy

Using the wind to propel a boat is magical, but it does take some skill. If you get it wrong, you might get wet! So be sure to go for your first sail with someone who is an experienced sailor. He or she will help you learn the basics, and take over when it's time for more difficult maneuvers.

A bit of theory
A sailboat isn't usually pushed along by the wind. In fact, as the sail is blown into a curved shape, it behaves like an aircraft wing, providing the "lift" that pulls the boat along. So the wind doesn't have to blow from behind the boat—you sail fastest when it blows from the side.

Getting started
With the wind blowing from the side, take the controls from your friend. Center the tiller (which steers the boat) and pull the sail in. As the wind fills the sail, the boat will start moving forward. Slowly let the sail out until it starts flapping and then pull it in a little until it stops. You're sailing!

Sit on the side across from the sail to balance the boat.

Turn around
Push the tiller away from you so that the boat turns around. The sail will move across the boat, and so must you! Duck your head and swap sides. Straighten out and sail back the way you came.

When the boat turns into the wind, it will slow down and may stop, so get some speed first.

Watch the front of the sail. If it goes slack, pull the tiller toward you until the sail fills again.

Beat . . .
To sail in the direction that the wind is coming from, you have to go in a series of zigzags. First head upwind at about 45 degrees to the wind direction. You have to pull the sail in almost as far as it will go and lean out more to stop the boat from blowing over. This is called beating. If you head too far upwind, the boat will stop, so be careful how you steer.

You will need to change sides and quickly pull the sail tight to keep the boat moving.

Wind direction

. . . then tack
Steer the boat into the wind and turn through 90 degrees, changing sides while ducking to avoid the sail. This is called tacking. Keep sailing as before, but this time with the wind against the other side of the boat. Then tack again in the other direction so that you zigzag upwind.

Swap with your friend
When you've had enough, tack again and then pull the tiller toward you, letting the sail out as you go, until you are sailing with the wind blowing from the side. Then let your friend take over.

Let the sail out to stop the boat before you swap.

THE PARTS OF A DINGHY

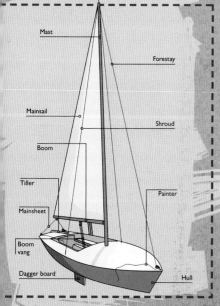

- Mast
- Forestay
- Mainsail
- Shroud
- Boom
- Tiller
- Painter
- Mainsheet
- Boom vang
- Dagger board
- Hull

177

Surf a wave

Get yourself a surfboard, learn a little surf slang, and head for the beach. If the surf's up, and you're pretty sure there are no sharks, it's time to get out there! Here's the basic technique for getting up onto a board, but the best thing to do is join a surf school where an instructor can watch and give you tips to improve your style.

Start in a low crouch to keep your center of gravity (balancing point) close to the board.

Boards come in several different designs—a soft foam board is best for beginners because it's safe and stable.

1 Walk into the water with your board. When you are stomach deep, climb onto the board and lie flat. Find a good balance so that the nose of the board is just above the water. Extend your legs with your feet out of the water and paddle out.

2 Use the "turtle roll" to get past breaking waves. When a wave approaches, grab the sides of the board and roll over so that the bottom of the board faces upward. Keep your chest close to the board. When you roll back up, the wave will have passed.

3 Watch for a small breaking wave rolling in from the ocean, and then point your board toward the beach, lie flat on your stomach, and paddle hard! Don't try to stand up; simply feel how the board moves when it rides a wave. Do this a few times.

4 Now try to catch a wave. Paddle back out, sit on your board, and watch as the waves roll in, crest, and break. As a wave starts to crest, point your board toward the shore and start paddling. You should start to feel like you're gliding on the wave.

Want to try surfing on snow? Turn to pages 170–171 to find out about snowboarding.

Ride a bodyboard

A bodyboard is designed for surfing while lying down and is much shorter than a surfboard. It's a great way to get into surfing—here's how to take off!

The unbroken wave is the part you're going to be riding.

1. Put your board in the water and lie on it with your hips along the back edge. Rest your elbows on the board as you paddle out using both your hands and feet.

2. Duck dive beneath oncoming waves. Paddle and kick as fast as you can as a wave approaches and, just as it is about to hit you, grip the front of the board and push the nose underwater. Place your knees on the back and apply your weight to submerge the board.

3. As the wave crashes overhead, hold on but let your knees come off the tail. As your body flattens out, you will pop up to the surface. Start paddling while waiting for the next wave.

4. When you are ready, catch a wave. You need one that has not broken but that is steep enough to push you hard. When it's about 5 ft (1.5 m) away, turn around and paddle as hard as you can to match its speed. Lean forward to accelerate and you're off!

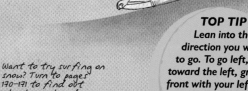

TOP TIP
Lean into the direction you want to go. To go left, lean toward the left, grab the front with your left hand, and plant your left elbow on the upper left side of the board.

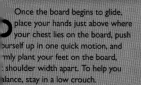

5. Once the board begins to glide, place your hands just above where your chest lies on the board, push yourself up in one quick motion, and firmly plant your feet on the board, shoulder width apart. To help you balance, stay in a low crouch.

6. Once you have your balance, you can start to rise out of the crouch position and begin riding. As you move into the standing position, your weight will drive the board to create extra speed. When you're doing this, you're a surfer!

Volley with water

Volleyball takes on a different dimension with this water sport. Perfect for soaking friends on summer days, see who can remain the driest and win the tournament. Each balloon burst by a team is a point for the other side. Let the volleying begin!

Water-filled balloons

2 large towels

3 friends

Badminton net or rope (optional)

TOP TIP
Fill up several water balloons and place them in a bucket to use when they are needed.

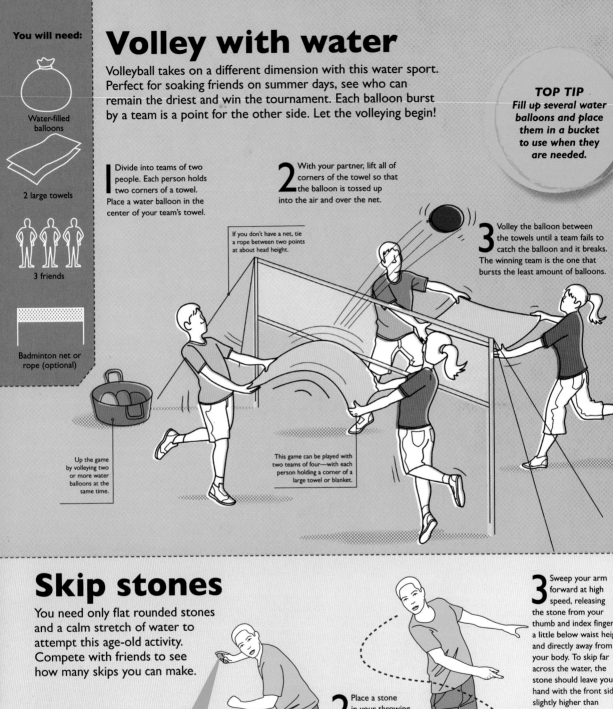

1 Divide into teams of two people. Each person holds two corners of a towel. Place a water balloon in the center of your team's towel.

2 With your partner, lift all of corners of the towel so that the balloon is tossed up into the air and over the net.

3 Volley the balloon between the towels until a team fails to catch the balloon and it breaks. The winning team is the one that bursts the least amount of balloons.

If you don't have a net, tie a rope between two points at about head height.

Up the game by volleying two or more water balloons at the same time.

This game can be played with two teams of four—with each person holding a corner of a large towel or blanket.

Skip stones

You need only flat rounded stones and a calm stretch of water to attempt this age-old activity. Compete with friends to see how many skips you can make.

1 Find an area of still water and collect some skipping stones. The best skipping stones have rounded edges, are flat on both sides, and can fit in the palm of your hand.

Flat, oval palm-size stones are perfect for skipping.

2 Place a stone in your throwing hand so that your thumb holds the stone on its front edge and your index finger curves along the bottom of the rear edge. Pull your arm behind you.

3 Sweep your arm forward at high speed, releasing the stone from your thumb and index finger a little below waist height and directly away from your body. To skip far across the water, the stone should leave your hand with the front side slightly higher than the rear.

Aim to hit the water's surface with the stone at a 10–20 degree angle.

Dive like an arrow

Diving into the water without making a splash is an impressive achievement. Follow these steps to make an elegant entrance into the pool.

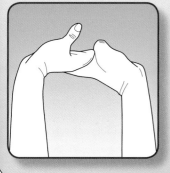

1 Place your right arm over your head with the palm of your hand pointing upward. Grab the back of your right hand with your left hand and hold the right palm flat.

2 Push your arms straight up so that your muscles are stretched tight. Your upper arms should be flat against your head, covering your ears.

Tensing all of your muscles creates stability that gives the water less chance to twist your body when you hit the surface.

3 To dive, jump into the water, tensing all of the muscles in your body so that you flow straight through the surface without making a splash.

This dive is also called "rip entry" because it sounds like a piece of paper being ripped as you hit the water.

Find out how to make a water bomb you can throw on pages 66–67.

Make a big splash

On a hot day, there's nothing more inviting than diving into cool water. For maximum impact, try a cannonball dive, which will create a loud splash that can heard all around the pool.

1 After checking that there are no people below you in the pool, jump off the edge.

2 Curl your knees up to your chest and tightly hold them there with both arms.

Safety!
Make sure that there are no obstructions, such as rocks, in the water below. Check that the water is deep enough to dive into without hitting the bottom.

3 With your legs tucked in, hit the water with your bottom and create a huge splash!

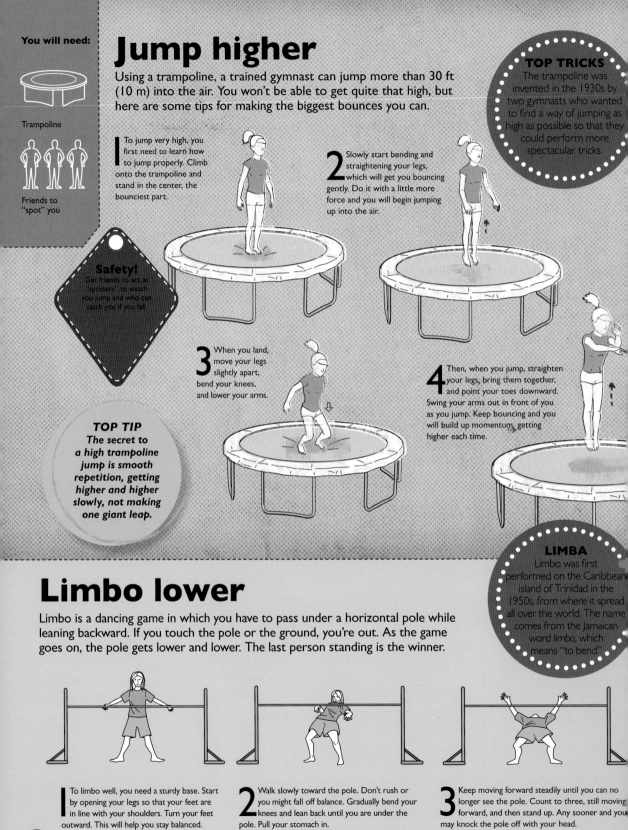

Jump higher

Using a trampoline, a trained gymnast can jump more than 30 ft (10 m) into the air. You won't be able to get quite that high, but here are some tips for making the biggest bounces you can.

Trampoline

Friends to "spot" you

TOP TRICKS
The trampoline was invented in the 1930s by two gymnasts who wanted to find a way of jumping as high as possible so that they could perform more spectacular tricks.

1 To jump very high, you first need to learn how to jump properly. Climb onto the trampoline and stand in the center, the bounciest part.

2 Slowly start bending and straightening your legs, which will get you bouncing gently. Do it with a little more force and you will begin jumping up into the air.

Safety!
Get friends to act as "spotters" to watch you jump and who can catch you if you fall.

3 When you land, move your legs slightly apart, bend your knees, and lower your arms.

4 Then, when you jump, straighten your legs, bring them together, and point your toes downward. Swing your arms out in front of you as you jump. Keep bouncing and you will build up momentum, getting higher each time.

TOP TIP
The secret to a high trampoline jump is smooth repetition, getting higher and higher slowly, not making one giant leap.

LIMBA
Limbo was first performed on the Caribbean island of Trinidad in the 1950s, from where it spread all over the world. The name comes from the Jamaican word *limba*, which means "to bend."

Limbo lower

Limbo is a dancing game in which you have to pass under a horizontal pole while leaning backward. If you touch the pole or the ground, you're out. As the game goes on, the pole gets lower and lower. The last person standing is the winner.

1 To limbo well, you need a sturdy base. Start by opening your legs so that your feet are in line with your shoulders. Turn your feet outward. This will help you stay balanced.

2 Walk slowly toward the pole. Don't rush or you might fall off balance. Gradually bend your knees and lean back until you are under the pole. Pull your stomach in.

3 Keep moving forward steadily until you can no longer see the pole. Count to three, still moving forward, and then stand up. Any sooner and you may knock the pole off with your head.

DIY mini golf

It's easy to make your own miniature golf course using whatever you happen to have lying around. You don't even need a golf club or a golf ball—a tennis racket (or perhaps a stick with a piece of sponge stuck to the end) and a plastic ball will be fine.

How to play

1 The goal of the game is to get your ball from the start to the hole in the fewest number of shots.

2 On your way around the three holes, you must hit the ball over, under, through, or against each of the obstacles along the way.

3 Note down the number of shots you take for each hole. See if you can reduce the number the next time around.

First hole
This hole has many obstacles. Don't hit your first shot too hard or you may find that your next one is impossible.

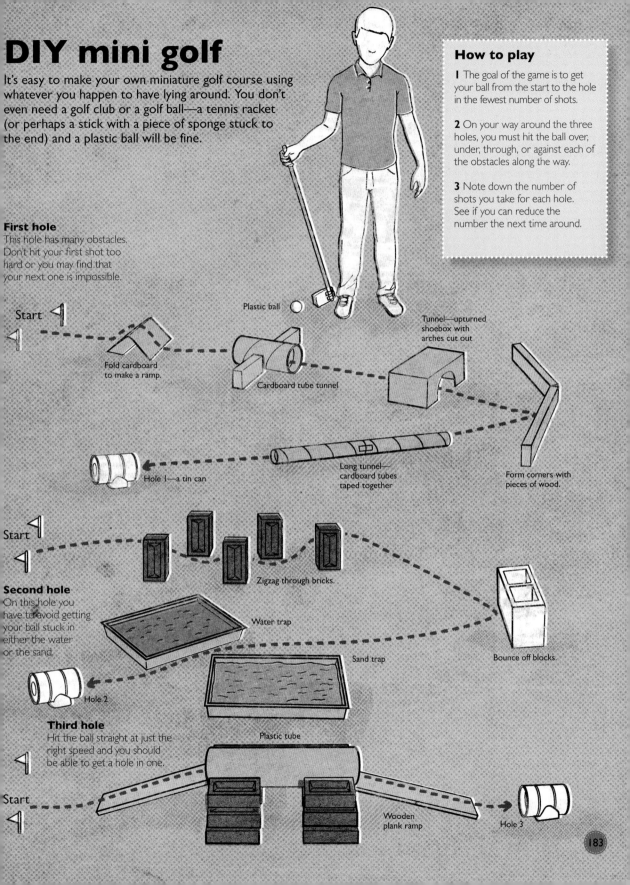

Plastic ball

Start

Fold cardboard to make a ramp.

Cardboard tube tunnel

Tunnel—upturned shoebox with arches cut out

Long tunnel—cardboard tubes taped together

Form corners with pieces of wood.

Hole 1—a tin can

Start

Zigzag through bricks.

Second hole
On this hole you have to avoid getting your ball stuck in either the water or the sand.

Water trap

Sand trap

Bounce off blocks.

Hole 2

Third hole
Hit the ball straight at just the right speed and you should be able to get a hole in one.

Plastic tube

Start

Wooden plank ramp

Hole 3

183

Master yo-yo tricks

These yo-yo throwing tricks follow on from one another. Mastering one will help you learn the next, building up to a cool trick.

TOP TIP
Try to use a good-quality yo-yo that "sleeps" (spins without moving) at the end of its string rather than coming right back.

The throwdown

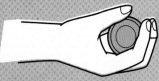

1 Place the yo-yo on its edge in the center of your palm with the string curling over the top of it. Attach the looped end of the string to your middle finger.

2 Flick your wrist and "throw" the yo-yo to the floor. When it reaches the end of the string, give a small jerk and the yo-yo will shoot back up. Turn your hand over and catch it in your palm.

The forward pass

1 Start off as you did with the throwdown, except this time with your hand hanging down by your side and the yo-yo behind you.

2 With a good, firm flick, throw the yo-yo straight out in front of you. When it gets to the end of its journey, yank it and the yo-yo will come shooting back. Catch it in your hand.

Around the world

1 The first part of this trick is identical to the forward pass, but when the yo-yo reaches the end of its string, instead of pulling it back, jerk your wrist upward and spin the yo-yo around in a 360-degree loop.

2 When the yo-yo has completed a full circle, tug the string and pull the yo-yo so it shoots back to your hand.

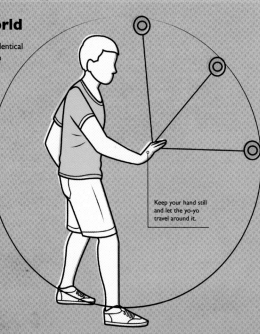

Keep your hand still and let the yo-yo travel around it.

Win at arm wrestling

You don't have to be super strong to win at arm wrestling. Although strength does help, there are a few tricks you can use to get the better of your opponent.

1 Grip your opponent's hand as high up as possible. When getting ready to wrestle, move your elbow forward so that your wrist is higher than his.

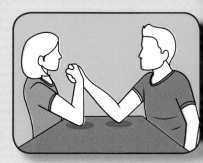

2 When the wrestling starts, roll your wrist toward you, which will bend your opponent's wrist back, making it hard for him to push your arm down.

3 Don't just try to push your opponent's hand straight down. Instead, pull his arm toward you. This allows you to gain leverage and use more strength.

Knuckle down at marbles

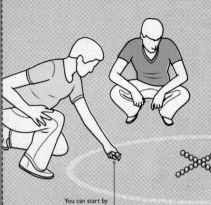

In a classic game of marbles, players use a large marble, known as a "shooter," to knock smaller marbles out of a circle. Whoever knocks out the most marbles wins. To achieve the difficult and most accurate shots, marble players use a technique called "knuckling down."

You will need:

Length of string

Chalk

Small marbles

2 large "shooter" marbles

You can start by randomly scattering the marbles if you prefer.

See if you can knock out more than one marble at a time.

1 To start, tie the chalk to one end of the string, and ask a friend to hold the other end. Pull the string out straight from them and draw a circle on the ground as you walk around. Place the small marbles in the middle of the circle.

2 Turn your shooting hand so that the palm faces upward. Place the shooter on your first two fingers. Curl your index finger around the shooter, holding it tight. Curl your other fingers up behind the shooter.

3 Place the knuckles of your shooting hand on the ground at the edge of the circle—this is knuckling down. Take aim at one of the marbles in the circle. When you're ready, use your thumb to flick the shooter at the marble.

4 If you knock a marble out of the circle, you get another turn. You must now knuckle down at the point where your shooter came to rest. As soon as you miss, it's your opponent's turn.

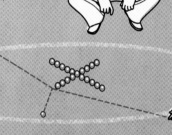

Play table soccer

Some of the best games are the simplest. All you need to play this version of table soccer are some coins, your hands, and an opponent.

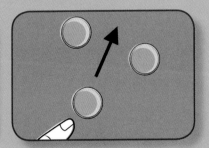

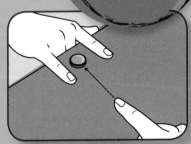

TOP TIP
Be careful not to flick too hard. Plan where you want your coins to be and carefully judge your flicks.

1 To score a goal, you must gradually flick your coins to the goal on the other side of the table. Arrange the coins in a triangle at the edge of the table, with one coin hanging halfway off the edge. To start, flick the end coin, which will separate the other two coins.

2 Flick the coin closest to you through the other two coins. If you miss your shot, hit one of the other coins, or if your coin goes off the table, it's your opponent's turn. Move across the table—you can pass only the closest coin to you through the other two.

3 When you reach the goal, you can take a shot. Your opponent forms a goal using their index finger and pinkie. If you move your coin between them, you get a point. Next, your opponent starts the game again from their side of the table.

Impress with world facts

Do you want to impress your family and friends with incredible facts about planet Earth? Well, here you can find mind-boggling records on everything from the world's oldest tree and deepest lake to the driest place and deadliest earthquake.

EUROPE

The **smallest country** in the world is **Vatican City** in Italy. It has an area of only 0.2 sq miles (0.4 sq km) and an official population of just **890 people**.

France is the world's most **popular vacation destination**, receiving more than 82 million tourists each year.

Russia is the **largest country** in the world. It is **70 times** as large as the U.K. and covers **11 percent** of Earth's total land surface.

The most **densely populated** country in the world is **Monaco**, with 43,830 people per sq mile (16,400 per sq km).

Lake Baikal in Siberia, Russia, is the world's **deepest and oldest lake**. It is 25 million years old, and parts of it are 5,712 ft (1,741 m) deep.

The world's **largest hot spring** is at **Deildartunguhver** in Iceland. This boiling river produces **40 gallons** (180 liters) of hot water per second.

The city of **Venice** in Italy is built on 118 islands dotted around a swampy marsh called the **Venetian Lagoon**.

ASIA

The world's **largest continent**, **Asia** covers one third of Earth's total land area.

Indonesia contains about **13,000 islands**, making it the largest **archipelago** (chain of islands) in the world.

Mongolia is the **most sparsely populated** country in the world, with only 4.4 people per sq mile (1.7 per sq km).

The **tallest building** in the world is the **Burj Khalifa** in Dubai, at a height of **2,559 ft** (780 m).

The world's deadliest **earthquake** took place in **Senshi province**, China, in 1556. More than 830,000 people perished in the disaster.

China and **India** both have more than one billion inhabitants. China, the world's **most populated country**, is home to one-fifth of the human race.

The world's **longest beach** is **Cox's Bazar** in Bangladesh, which stretches for **75 miles** (120 km).

Cherrapunji in northeastern India is the **wettest place** on Earth, receiving an annual rainfall of **500 in** (1,270 cm).

NORTH AMERICA

Greenland is the **largest island** in the world (after Australia, which is regarded as a continent rather than an island). It has an area of **836,109 sq miles** (2,133,986 sq km)—yet only 56,000 people live there.

Mexico City, North America's **most populated city**, is home to more than 20,450,000 people.

The **Grand Canyon** in Colorado is the **largest land gorge** in the world, extending for more than **220 miles** (350 km) and measuring 18 miles (29 km) **at its widest point.**

Established in 1872 in the states of Wyoming, Montana, and Idaho is **Yellowstone National Park**, the world's **oldest national park**.

The **largest living tree** is a 3,500-year-old giant sequoia called **General Sherman**. Located in the Sequoia National Park, California, it is 271 ft (82.6 m) tall and weighs **2,200 tonnes**.

The world's **highest cliffs** are the sea cliffs on the island of Molokai, Hawaii. These towering rocks rise **3,300 ft** (1,010 m) above the shore.

With a height of only **43 ft** (13 m), **Cuexcomate** in Mexico is the world's **smallest volcano**.

The world's **longest cave system** is **Mammoth Cave** in Kentucky, which extends for more than **367 miles** (590 km) and is home to more than 130 species of wildlife.

SOUTH AMERICA

The *driest place* in the world is the **Atacama Desert** in Chile. Some parts of the desert have had no rain for **400 years.**

Brazil is the *largest country* in South America and covers almost half of the *total area* of the continent.

Venezuela is home to the world's *highest waterfall.* **Angel Falls** in Canaima National Park has a total drop of 3,212 ft (979 m).

The Amazon is the world's widest river—reaching widths of up to **7 miles** (11 km). The river contains about **2,500 species of fish**—more than there are in the Atlantic Ocean.

Bolivia's capital, **La Paz**, founded by the Spanish in 1548, is the *highest capital city* in the world, at an altitude of 11,916 ft (3,682 m).

The **Andes,** the world's *longest mountain range*, is 7,200 miles (4,500 km) long and crosses **seven** countries. It is home to **Aconcagua,** the world's *highest volcano*, with a height of 22,831 ft (6,960 m).

AFRICA

With an area of 966,749 sq miles (2,504,530 sq km), **Sudan** is *the largest country* in Africa.

The **Nile**, the world's *longest river*, extends 4,160 miles (6,695 km). It has *frozen over* twice in recorded history, once in the **800s** and again in the **1000s.**

The **Sahara**, the largest hot desert in the world, covers one third of the area of Africa. It is roughly **16 times** the size of France.

Kericho in Kenya has an average of **132 days** *of hail each year.*

Nigeria is the most *densely populated* country in Africa, with more than **145 million people.**

About **45 percent** of Africa's population is aged *15 or under.*

Mount Kilimanjaro, an extinct volcano in Tanzania, is Africa's *highest peak* at 19,341 ft (5,895 m).

The **highest temperature** ever recorded is 135.8°F (57.7°C) at **Al Aziziyah** in the Sahara Desert, Libya, on September 13, 1922.

OCEANIA

Australia is the largest country in Oceania, with a population of more than **21 million** people.

Mount Wilhelm in Papua New Guinea is Oceania's *highest mountain* at 14,793 ft (4,509 m).

About **820 languages** are spoken in **Papua New Guinea**—more than in any other country in the world.

The **Great Barrier Reef**, situated off the coast of Queensland, Australia, is the *largest living structure* on Earth. It extends 1,250 miles (2,010 km) and is made up of more than 3,000 reefs.

The *smallest country* in Oceania is the Pacific island of **Nauru**, with an area of only **8 sq miles** (21 sq km). It is the only country in the world that has *no capital city*.

Australia has about **880 reptile species**—more than any other country in the world.

ANTARCTICA

Antarctica is the world's *driest continent.* It receives less than **2 in** (5 cm) of rainfall each year, and some of its valleys have had no rain for *four million years.*

The **permanent population** of Antarctica is about **1,000 research scientists**. That number rises to 5,000 during the summer.

During the winter, the area of *frozen seawater* around Antarctica roughly **doubles in size** to 7.2 million sq miles (20 million sq km)—that's *one and a half times the size of the U.S.*

The **Ross Ice Shelf**—the *largest ice shelf* in the world—is almost twice the size of the U.K.

98 percent of the **land surface** of Antarctica is covered by **ice.**

The *lowest temperature* ever recorded was -128.5°F (-89.2°C) at **Vostok research station,** Antarctica, on July 21, 1983.

The world's *windiest place* is Port Martin, Antarctica, with an average wind speed of 108 mph (174 km/h).

If Antarctica's **ice sheets** melted, the *world's oceans* would rise by an estimated 210 ft (65 m).

Amaze with world trivia

If you want to amaze people with your astonishing knowledge of world trivia, this is the place to find awe-inspiring facts such as how big the largest snowflake was, which country has the biggest spider, or where you can find the world's largest swimming pool.

EUROPE

Eyeglasses were first worn in *Italy* in about *1285*.

The **Swiss** are the world's biggest *chocolate fans*, consuming 24 lb (11 kg) per head each year.

The *people of Andorra* have the *highest life expectancy* in the world, with an average of *83.5 years*.

The **first highway** opened in **Germany** in *1932*. On many German highways, there is *no speed limit.*

Heathrow Airport, U.K., is the world's *busiest airport* in terms of international passenger numbers. *66,036,957* passengers passed through its doors in 2009.

The flag of **Denmark**, dating back to the 1200s, is the world's *oldest unchanged national flag.*

The largest **traffic jam** took place in France on February 16, 1980. It stretched *109 miles* (176 km) from Paris to Lyon and involved more than *200,000* vehicles.

ASIA

The world's largest commercial employer is **Indian Railways**, with *1.65 million* employees. It transports more than *six billion* people every year.

The Japanese own an estimated *19 million pets*. There are more pets in Japan than there are children under 15.

One **child** is born in **India** every *1.26 seconds*.

When **Krakatoa**—a volcanic island in *Indonesia*—erupted in 1883, the blast could be heard *2,983 miles* (4,800 km) away.

The **cobra**, one of the most venomous snakes on Earth, kills more than *7,000 people* each year in India.

The Indonesian island of **Sumatra** is home to the **world's heaviest flower**. The *Rafflesia arnoldii*, weighs up to 15 lb (7 kg) and can grow to the size of an umbrella.

More people own **Rolls-Royces** in Hong Kong than anywhere else in the world.

The **imperial throne of Japan** has been occupied by the same family for the past *1,300 years*.

NORTH AMERICA

The **United States** and **Russia** are less than 5 miles (3 km) apart at their closest point.

The **Chihuahua**, the world's smallest dog, is named after a state in Mexico.

The biggest library in the world is the **Library of Congress** in Washington, D.C. It contains about *28 million* books.

Every year, the **U.S. Postal Service** handles an estimated *800,000* letters addressed to Santa Claus, North Pole.

The U.S. consumes *25 percent* of the world's energy.

The *largest snowflakes* ever recorded fell on January 28, 1887 in Fort Keogh, Montana. These giant flakes were 15 in (38 cm) in diameter and 8 in (20 cm) thick.

564 Native American tribes are officially recognized in the U.S., although the current Native American population is less than *one percent* of the U.S.'s total population.

The **Ice Hotel** in Québec, Canada, is created every year using *400 tons* of ice and *12,000 tons* of snow. It melts every summer and is recreated every winter.

By 2020, **China** is expected to be the *most visited country* in the world.

Shinsegae Centum City in South Korea is the world's *largest department store.*

SOUTH AMERICA

The world's biggest carnival parade is the *Galo da Madrugada* in **Brazil**—it attracts more than 1,500,000 people each year.

The **Quechua Indians** of South America have more than **1,000** different names for **potatoes**.

There is only *one movie theater* in all of **Suriname**, a country in northern South America with a population of *481,267.*

The world's *largest swimming pool* is the **San Alfonso del Mar** in Algarrobo, Chile. This vast seawater pool is 3,324 ft (1,013 m) long—that's larger than *15 football fields.*

Argentines eat more **meat** than any other nation.

The *world's biggest spider* is the **Goliath bird-eating spider** of South America. It measures 11 in (27.9 cm) in diameter and eats birds, snakes, lizards, and bats.

One third of the **world's rainforests** are in **Brazil**.

AFRICA

Of the **Seven Wonders of the Ancient World**, only the *pyramids of Giza* in Egypt still remain.

Discovered in *South Africa* in 1905, the world's **largest diamond**, named *The Cullinan*, weighed 3,106 carats.

Libya is the only country in the world to have a *single color* on its **flag** (green).

There are **223 pyramids** in **Sudan**—85 more than in Egypt.

The people of **Swaziland** have the *shortest life expectancy*. The average life expectancy for both men and women is just *30.8 years.*

The **Republic of South Africa** has more *official languages* than any other country—11 in total.

A hyena's laugh can reach its clan members *3 miles* (5 km) away.

Hippopotamuses kill more people in Africa than any other animal—usually by *trampling on them*.

OCEANIA

The world's *biggest movie screen* is the **IMAX** in **Sydney**, Australia. It is 96 ft (29 m) high by 117 ft (35 m) wide and covers an area of more than 10,925 sq ft (1,015 sq m).

There are *58 million kangaroos* in Australia—more than twice the number of humans.

The largest **gold nugget** ever found weighed 158 lb (72 kg). It was discovered during the 1869 gold rush in Moliagul, Australia.

There are **15,000 bush fires** in Australia every year. In 2009, the "Black Saturday" fires in the southern Australian state of Victoria caused more than *200 deaths*.

From November to May, Australia's coastal waters are home to the world's most **poisonous jellyfish**. The box jellyfish, *Chironex fleckeri*, carries enough venom to kill *60 humans*.

In 1873, **New Zealand** became the first independent nation to give women the **right to vote** in national elections.

ANTARCTICA

At the **South Pole** there is **no sunshine** for 182 days each year.

During the feeding season in Antarctica, a blue whale eats about **four million krill** (shrimplike creatures) per day—that's 8,000 lb (3,600 kg) every day for *six months*.

On January 7, 1978, **Emilio Marcos Palma** was the first person to be **born** in Antarctica.

Antarctica is **not owned** by any country. The **Antarctic Treaty**, signed by 46 countries, states that the continent should be used only for *scientific research*.

The **thickest ice** ever recorded was found in **Wilkes Land** in Antarctica in 1975. It was *15,669 ft* (4,776 m) deep—that's equivalent to *10 Empire State Buildings*.

Antarctica's **largest land animal** is a species of **midge** that is only *0.5 in* (12 mm) long.

Index

Credits

DK would like to thank:
Hazel Beynon, Samone Bos, Joe Fullman,
Julie Kamel, Ashwin Khurana, Victoria
Heywood-Dunne, and Andrea Mills for
editorial assistance. Daniela Boraschi,
Spencer Holbrook, Phil Letsu, Smiljka
Surla, Jacqui Swan, and Jane Thomas for
help with design. Darren Awuah for
illustrations. Stefan Podhorodecki for
photography. Nic Dean for picture
research. Lucy Claxton and Romaine
Werblow in the DK Picture Library.
Stephanie Pliakas for proofreading. Jackie
Brind for the index. Sam Buckmaster, Josie
Firmin, Rowan Firmin, Claire Collins for
making the crafts. St John's Ambulance for
checking the First Aid spreads.

**The publisher would like to thank
the following for their kind
permission to reproduce their
photographs:**

(Key: a-above; b-below/bottom; c-centre;
f-far; l-left; r-right; t-top)

Alamy Images: Bryan and Cherry
Alexander / Arcticphoto 134ca;
Blickwinkel / Menz 97tl; David Forster
150fbl; Marni Garfat 162tr; Bob Gibbons
93tr; David Northcott / Danita Delimont,
Agent 129fcl; Phototake Inc. / Richard T.
Nowitz 96tr; Jeff Rotman 127b; Michael
Runkel Utah 173cr. **Ardea:** Kenneth W.
Fink 129cla. **Corbis:** 117bl; Wong Adam /
Redlink 93cla; Neil Beer 29bc; Fernando
Bengoechea / Beateworks 70-71
(background); Edward Bock 167tl; Sam
Diephuis / Zefa 70tl; Beat Glanzmann
134-135; Liz Hafalia / San Francisco
Chronicle 17tr; Jon Hicks 38-39; Klaus
Honal / Naturfoto Honal 93tl; Illustration
Works 95cb; Didrik Johnck 175tr; Danilo
Krstanovic / Reuters 75tr; Steve Lupton
47t; Joe McDonald 127t, 129c; Charlie
Munsey 176b; David A. Northcott 129cl;
William Perlman / Star Ledger 31cra;
Murray Richards / Icon SMI 178-179;
Andersen Ross / Blend Images 39tr; Galen
Rowell 174-175; Paul Thompson 105t;

Onne van der Wal 177ftr; Michael S.
Yamashita 109fbr. **Dorling Kindersley:**
Natural History Museum, London 105fcra
(tooth), 105ftr (belemnite shell); Pitt
Rivers Museum, University of Oxford
105crb; Rough Guides / Gavin Thomas
156b. **FLPA:** Derek Middleton 150bl;
Chris and Tilde Stuart 150br. **Galaxy
Picture Library:** Robin Scagell 118cla,
118cra. **Getty Images:** AFP Photo / Don
Emmert 37b; Asia Images / Wang Leng
59c; Aurora / Menno Boermans 173ca;
Walter Hodges / Stone 146-147; Iconica /
Philip and Karen Smith 84bl; The Image
Bank / Seth Joel 35br; Clive Nichols / GAP
Photos 93cra; Nordic Photos / Jan Rietz
56ca; StockFood Creative / Renee Comet
43t; Stone / Terje Rakke 56-57; Stone /
Wayne R Bilenduke 135cr; Tim Graham
Photo Library 109br; Visuals Unlimited /
Dr. James Richardson 103br.
iStockphoto.com: 77studio 56-57b;
AntiMartina 69fcl; John Bell 128bl;
Michelle Bennett / Jeanniemay 72tr; Karel
Broz 128cr; Kjell Brynildsen 69cl; Alena
Dvorakova 128cl; Giorgio Fochesato
151bc; Cheryl Graham 164tr; Bill Grove
84bc; Eileen Hart 84br, 84fbr; id-work
26-27c; Marcus Lindström 85br, 85crb;
Mandygodbehear 154t; Slobo Mitic 128tr;
Alex Potemkin 57cr; Jacom Stephens
84ca, 84t; TrilingStudio 26c; Vika Valter

85bl; Tomasz Zachariasz 128c, 128ca.
Mary Evans Picture Library:
Illustrated London News Ltd. 34crb.
NASA: GRC 117cl; JPL 116-117, 117clb;
JSC 115, 117cla. **naturepl.com:** Philippe
Clement 151fbl; Gavin Maxwell 150fbr.
NHPA / Photoshot: A.N.T. Photo
Library 129bc, 129bl; Anthony Bannister
129ca; John Cancalosi 129fcla; Stephen
Dalton 94cra; Daniel Heuclin 129fbl.
Science Photo Library: 32cla, 33tl;
Adam Hart-Davis 110-111; Lawrence
Lawry 106-107, 107tr; John Sanford 119b;
Jerry Schad 119t; Eckhard Slawik 118ca.
TopFoto.co.uk: Peter Hvizdak / The
Image Works 125br; Keystone 88-89.